A CELEBRATION OF
CATS

By the same author:

NAKED AS THE GLASS. October House, N.Y.
JOURNEY TOWARD POETRY. October House, N.Y.

A CELEBRATION OF CATS

an anthology of poems

Compiled and Edited by
JEAN BURDEN

PAUL S. ERIKSSON, INC. *New York*

 Published simultaneously in Canada by George J. McLeod, Ltd., Toronto, Ontario. Library of Congress Catalog Card Number 74-80960. ISBN 0-8397-1336-3.
Manufactured in the United States of America.

Book design by Wanda Lubelska/Ben Feder, Inc.

Acknowledgements

The New Yorker Magazine, Inc.: "Looking for Itsy" by Naomi Lazard, reprinted by permission; © 1971 The New Yorker Magazine, Inc. "Walking with Lulu in the Wood" by Naomi Lazard, reprinted by permission; © 1969 The New Yorker Magazine, Inc. "Catalog" by Rosalie Moore, reprinted by permission; © 1940, 1968 The New Yorker Magazine, Inc. "Winter Tryst" by Ormonde de Kay, reprinted by permission; © 1958 The New Yorker Magazine, Inc. (Continued on page 213).

In memory of my cat, Beckett—
familiar of light and dark

CONTENTS

2. DEMONIC

3. MYSTERIOUS

4. ANTIC

5. WILD

6. UNDEFINED

PREFACE

Poetry and cats have always had a strange affinity. Why not poetry and dogs? Or poetry and parakeets?

As a poet and notorious ailurophile, I have long pondered the question. When I finally came to compile this anthology, I determined to try to find the answer.

Cat. The word carries on its back a fascinating load of associations, history, romance, myth and symbol. It brings with it not only the physical image of *Felis catus*, but of his wild ancestors that stalked their prey in dim jungles and thick grasses. Of all domesticated animals, the cat seems to have changed the least from his primitive self. Prowling his own quiet backyard or asleep by the fire, he is still only a whisker away from the wilds. A purr can change instantly into a snarl; a love-pat into a predator's swipe. All this is part of the magnetism, but only part. A cat, it would seem, is always more than just a cat.

Can we pin down the mysterious attraction, the power, beauty, charm, appeal—and sometimes the opposite—the revulsion and dread which some people feel toward cats? As a matter of fact, one is seldom indifferent to the word *cat*: one is either strongly pro-cat or equally strongly anti-cat. Few people just don't mind cats. (And this goes for poets, as well.) Whatever rationalizations people give for their attitudes toward these creatures of the night, they usually hide irrational feelings emerging from much deeper levels of consciousness than mere common sense.

Why have fantastic powers from both black and white magic been attributed to the cat? Can the answer be found in the aura of myths and legends surrounding it? Or, perhaps, in its actual history?

The polarity of the angelic and demonic has characterized the cat ever since it crept out of the wild places of Africa into the home and daily life of the early Egyptians some five thousand years ago. It wasn't long before the cat became chief of Egypt's sacred animals, along with the baboon and crocodile. He was loved, cherished and protected—even worshipped. Anyone who was so foolish as to kill a cat was himself executed. Although the cat worked to protect Egyptian granaries from rodents, he was primarily a religious symbol, something to be adored for his grace and beauty. One of the popular Egyptian deities, the goddess Pasht, had a cat's head. When her temple was excavated many years ago, thousands and thousands of mummified cats were uncovered. This isn't as far a cry as one might think from the near-deification that some cats enjoy today, especially by lonely spinsters. They too are given fancy funerals and often left fortunes upon the death of their owners.

From worship to persecution—the cat's history has run the gamut. In the Middle Ages cats became associated with evil, and to some people they still are. In the 15th century, the cat came close to being run out of existence entirely. It started wih a lusty Norse goddess named Freya who rode in a chariot drawn by two black cats. Freya became the central figure in a Teutonic cult which, competing with Christianity, spread through western Europe. Predictably, a rival religion was feared and resented by the established church which in its ignorance and panic instituted witch hunts, torture and murder. No one knows how many thousands of humans—and cats—were put to death. A whisper of evidence—or merely hearsay—was enough to justify persecution, and ownership of a cat (particularly black) was proof of sorcery and the devil. This kind of insanity endured for years, spreading west to Great Britain and America, before the cat came into his own as mankind's beloved pet as well as its most conscientious vermin-hunter.

We finally discovered that the cat is neither divine nor diabolic, but a little of both, a loyal friend of man, guardian of his home and storehouse. All the elements of the cat's tapestried past, however, linger in the art surrounding him—in music, painting, sculpture, engravings, ballet—and poetry. Cat the hunter, the devil, the sorcerer, the incarnation of evil, exists side by side with the creature of angelic grace, the protector of the hearth, the hero of countless adventures. It is interesting, in passing, that the common designation of the cat as feminine rather than masculine is true when we are speaking of the cat as a symbol. Down through history the cat has been much more associated with feminine forms, such as the goddesses Pasht and Freya, than with masculine. Because its eyes dilate at night, it has also been identified with Diana, goddess of the moon. And it was witches who allegedly kept cats and were killed for the practice.

Poets have long recognized the cat's paradox, that he is what

Jung aptly called an archetypal image as well as an animal to pet, and as such carries a wealth of associations only explainable in psychological terms, in the language of the unconscious. The "beast" is a frequenter of dreams, embodying all kinds of primitive characteristics both good and bad. The cat is often that beast, grinning or snarling.

The cat first appeared in literature in fables. Except for a brief mention in an early Greek poem (c. A.D. 550), the cat's celebration in poetry is not featured until the 8th century when an unknown Irish monk at Reichenau wrote "Pangur Bán" in a commonplace book. As usual in those early days, the cat was vis à vis a mouse. Chaucer also wrote about a cat (and mouse), as did other 15th and 16th century poets that came after. But when Christopher Smart (1722–1771) was confined to Bedlam with his cat Jeoffry, he wrote of him as "the servant of the living God . . ./For he keeps the Lord's watch in the night against the adversary . . ./For he counteracts the Devil, who is death by brisking about the life . . ./For the Cherub Cat is a term of the Angel Tiger . . ."

This dichotomy between the cat as good and evil exists to the present day. At no other time has the cat been so celebrated in poetry as in the 20th century, and it is on these modern poems that this book is focused. The last anthology of cat poems (to my knowledge) was published in 1946. Only a portion of its verse was contemporary. Although our selections are, of course, uneven (true of all anthologies), we hope in this volume to have captured some of the finest poetry about cats of our time.

A dog, I have always said, is prose; a cat is a poem. Only those who do not like cats know all about them. Cats speak to poets in their natural tongue, and something profound and untamed in us answers.

I am indebted not only to the sources listed in "Acknowledgements," but to *Cat Fancy* magazine whose poetry page I had the pleasure of editing (under a pseudonym) for three years. I am also grateful to Ruth Munch for her help in tracking down the poems and their proper credits.

Jean Burden

Altadena, California
August, 1974

1.

ANGELIC

PANGUR BÁN

(Written by a student of the monastery of Corinthia on a copy of St. Paul's Epistles, in the eighth century.)

I and Pangur Bán, my cat,
'Tis a like task we are at:
Hunting mice is his delight,
Hunting words I sit all night.

Better far than praise of men
'Tis to sit with book and pen;
Pangur bears me no ill-will,
He too plies his simple skill.

'Tis a merry thing to see
At our tasks how glad are we,
When at home we sit and find
Entertainment to our mind.

Oftentimes a mouse will stray
In the hero Pangur's way;
Oftentimes my keen thought set
Takes a meaning in its net.

'Gainst the wall he sets his eye
Full and fierce and sharp and sly;
'Gainst the wall of knowledge I
All my little wisdom try.

When a mouse darts from its den,
O how glad is Pangur then!
O what gladness do I prove
When I solve the doubts I love!

So in peace our tasks we ply,
Pangur Bán, my cat, and I;
In our arts we find our bliss,
I have mine and he has his.

Practice every day has made
Pangur perfect in his trade;
I get wisdom day and night
Turning darkness into light.

Anon: *translated from the Gaelic by* Robin Flower

MY CAT JEOFFRY

For I will consider my Cat Jeoffry.
For he is the servant of the Living God, duly and daily serving him.
For at the first glance of the glory of God in the East he worships in his way.
For is this done by wreathing his body seven times round with elegant quickness.
For then he leaps up to catch the musk, which is the blessing of God upon his prayer.
For he rolls upon prank to work it in.
For having done duty and received blessing he begins to consider himself.
For this he performs in ten degrees.
For first he looks upon his fore-paws to see if they are clean.
For secondly he kicks up behind to clear away there.
For thirdly he works it upon stretch with the fore-paws extended.
For fourthly he sharpens his paws by wood.
For fifthly he washes himself.
For sixthly he rolls upon wash.
For seventhly he fleas himself, that he may not be interrupted upon the beat.
For eighthly he rubs himself against a post.
For ninthly he looks up for his instructions.
For tenthly he goes in quest of food.

For having consider'd God and himself he will consider his
neighbor.
For if he meets another cat he will kiss her in kindness.
For when he takes his prey he plays with it to give it a chance.
For one mouse in seven escapes by his dallying.
For when his day's work is done his business more properly begins.
For he keeps the Lord's watch in the night against the adversary.
For he counteracts the powers of darkness by his electrical skin &
glaring eyes.
For he counteracts the Devil, who is death, by brisking about the
life.
For in his morning orisons he loves the sun and the sun loves him.
For he is of the tribe of Tiger.
For the Cherub Cat is a term of the Angel Tiger.
For he has the subtlety and hissing of a serpent, which in goodness
he suppresses.
For he will not do destruction, if he is well-fed, neither will he spit
without provocation.
For he purrs in thankfulness, when God tells him he's a good Cat.
For he is an instrument for the children to learn benevolence upon.
For every house is incompleat without him & a blessing is lacking
in the spirit.

Christopher Smart

TO A CAT

I

Stately, lordly friend,
Condescend
Here to sit by me, and turn
Glorious eyes that smile and burn,
Golden eyes, love's lustrous meed,
On the golden page I read.

All your wondrous wealth of hair,
Dark and fair,
Silken-shaggy, soft and bright
As the clouds and beams of night,
Pays my reverent hand's caress
Back with friendlier gentleness.

Dogs may fawn on all and some
As they come;
You, a friend of loftier mind,
Answer friends alone in kind.
Just your foot upon my hand
Softly bids it understand

Morning round this silent sweet
Garden-seat
Sheds its wealth of gathering light,
Thrills the gradual clouds with might,
Changes woodland, orchard, heath,
Lawn, and garden there beneath.

Fair and dim they gleamed below:
Now they glow
Deep as even your sunbright eyes,
Fair as even the wakening skies.
Can it not or can it be
Now that you give thanks to see?

May not you rejoice as I,
Seeing the sky
Change to heaven revealed, and bid
Earth reveal the heaven it hid
All night long from stars and moon,
Now the sun sets all in tune?

What within you wakes with day
Who can say?
All too little may we tell,
Friends who like each other well,

What might haply, if we might,
Bid us read our lives aright.

II

Wild on woodland ways your sires
          Flashed like fires:
Fair as flame and fierce and fleet
As with wings on wingless feet
Shone and sprang your mother, free,
Bright and brave as wind or sea.
Free and proud and glad as they,
          Here to-day
Rests or roams their radiant child,
Vanquished not, but reconciled,
Free from curb of aught above
Save the lovely curb of love.

Love through dreams of souls divine
          Fain would shine
Round a dawn whose light and song
Then should right our mutual wrong—
Speak and seal the love-lit law
Sweet Assisi's seer foresaw.

Dreams were theirs; yet haply may
          Dawn a day
When such friends and fellows born,
Seeing our earth as fair at morn.
May for wiser love's sake see
More of heaven's deep heart than we.

Algernon Charles Swinburne

THE YOUNG CAT AND THE CHRYSANTHEMUMS

You mince, you start
advancing indirectly—
your tail upright
knocking about among the
frail heavily flowered
sprays.

Yes, you are lovely
with your ingratiating
manners, sleek sides and
small white paws, but
I wish you had not come
here.

William Carlos Williams

ON A CAT AGEING

He blinks upon the hearth-rug
And yawns in deep content,
Accepting all the comforts
That Providence has sent.

Louder he purrs and louder,
In one glad hymn of praise
For all the night's adventures,
For quiet, restful days.

Life will go on forever,
With all that cat can wish;
Warmth, and the glad procession
Of fish and milk and fish.

Only—the thought disturbs him—
He's noticed once or twice,
That times are somehow breeding
A nimbler race of mice.

Alexander Gray

LAST WORDS TO A DUMB FRIEND

Pet was never mourned as you,
Purrer of the spotless hue,
Plumy tail, and wistful gaze
While you humoured our queer ways,
Or outshrilled your morning call
Up the stairs and through the hall—
Foot suspended in its fall—
While, expectant you would stand
Arched, to meet the stroking hand;
Till your way you choose to wend
Yonder, to your tragic end.

Never another pet for me!
Let your place all vacant be;
Better blankness day by day
Than companion torn away.
Better bid his memory fade,
Better blot each mark he made,
Selfishly escape distress
By contrived forgetfulness,
Than preserve his prints to make
Every morn and eve an ache.

From the chair whereon he sat
Sweep his fur, nor wince thereat;
Rake his little pathway out
Mid the bushes roundabout;
Smooth away his talons' mark
From the claw-worn pine-tree bark,
Where he climbed as dusk embrowned,
Waiting us who loitered round.

Strange it is this speechless thing,
Subject to our mastering,
Subject for his life and food
To our gift, and time, and mood;
Timid pensioner of us Powers,
His existence ruled by ours,
Should—by crossing at a breath
Into safe and shielded death,
By the merely taking hence
Of his insignificance—
Loom as largened to the sense,
Shape as part, above man's will,
Of the Imperturbable.

As a prisoner, flight debarred,
Exercising in a yard,
Still retain I, troubled, shaken,
Mean estate, by him forsaken;
And this home, which scarcely took
Impress from his little look,
By his faring to the Dim
Grows all eloquent of him.

Housemate, I can think you still
Bounding to the window-sill,
Over which I vaguely see
Your small mound beneath the tree,
Showing in the autumn shade
That you moulder where you played.

Thomas Hardy

A CAT

Silently licking his gold-white paw
Oh gorgeous Celestino, for
God made lovely things, yet
Our lovely cat surpasses them all.
The gold, the iron, the waterfall,
The nut, the peach, apple, granite
Are lovely things to look at, yet,
Our lovely cat surpasses them all.

John Gittings
Age 8

PORTRAIT OF A YOUNG CAT

If you would know my cat: he moves like the wind in the reeds,
black as spilled ink and paper-white are his furs,
when he shakes his head, his eyes make a bright half-circle of beads.
At a touch, he explodes like a snapdragon into loud purrs.

Elizabeth J. Coatsworth

THE CAT IN THE WOOD

The cat in the wood cried farewell cried farewell
Farther and farther away and the leaves
Covered her over with sound of the leaves
And sound of the wood O my love O my love
Farther and farther away and the sound
Of leaves overhead when I call to you
Leaves on the ground.

Archibald MacLeish

EPITAPH FOR MY CAT

And now my pampered beast
who hated to be wet,
The rain falls all night
And you are under it.
Who liked to be so warm,
Are cold as any stone.
Who kept so clean and neat,
Cast down in the dirt
Of death's filthy sport.

Jean Garrigue

THE HAPPY CAT

The cat's asleep; I whisper *kitten*
Till he stirs a little and begins to purr—
He doesn't wake. Today out on the limb
(The limb he thinks he can't climb down from)
He mewed until I heard him in the house.
I climbed up to get him down: he mewed.
What he says and what he sees are limited.
My own response is even more constricted.
I think, "It's lucky; what you have is too."
What do you have except—well, me?
I joke about it but it's not a joke:
The house and I are all he remembers.
Next month how will he guess that it is winter
And not just entropy, the universe
Plunging at last into its cold decline?
I cannot think of him without a pang.
Poor rumpled thing, why don't you see
That you have no more, really, than a man?
Men aren't happy: why are you?

Randall Jarrell

MIDWIFE CAT

Beyond the fence she hesitates,
 And drops a paw, and tries the dust.
It is a clearing, but she waits
 No longer minute than she must.

Though a dozen foes may dart
 From out the grass, she crouches by,
Then runs to where the silos start
 To heave their shadows far and high.

Here she folds herself and sleeps;
 But in a moment she has put
The dreams aside; and now she creeps
 Across the open, foot by foot,

Till at the threshold of a shed
 She smells the water and the corn
Where a sow is on her bed
 And little pigs are being born.

Silently she leaps, and walks
 All night upon a narrow rafter,
Whence at intervals she talks
 Wise to them she watches after.

Mark Van Doren

A GARDEN-LION

O Michael, you are at once the enemy
And the chief ornament of our garden,
Scrambling up rose-posts, nibbling at nepeta,
Making your lair where tender plants should flourish,
Or proudly couchant on a sun-warmed stone.

What do you do all night there,
When we seek our soft beds,
And you go off, old roisterer,
Away into the dark?

I think you play at leopards and panthers;
I think you wander on to foreign properties;
But on winter mornings you are a lost orphan
Pitifully wailing underneath our windows;

And in summer, by the open doorway,
You come in pad, pad, lazily to breakfast,
Plumy tail waving, with a fine swagger,
Like a drum-major, or a parish beadle,
Or a rich rajah, or a Grand Mogul.

Evelyn Hayes

TO PUFFIN, A WHITE CAT

On the dark blue rug that is a midnight sky
The creamy saucer fills its heaven like a moon,
And over it a cat's white face
Basks in a muted ecstasy,
Lapping the milky way to paradise
With near-shut golden eyes, pearled beard and rosy mouth,
A cosy mask, lit by contentment from within
And by reflected radiance from beneath;
Where, like true benevolence, eclipsing its material cause,
The saucer, empty, still illuminates,
While Puffin sits and contemplates
Infinity's great O, the starry silk
Of dreams that only can be patched with milk.

Until the want is satisfied, for joy he softly roars,
And kneads his milky firmament with omnipresent paws.

James Kirkup

THE KITTEN IN THE FALLING SNOW

The year-old kitten
has never seen snow,
fallen or falling, until now
this late winter afternoon.

He sits with wide eyes
at the firelit window, sees
white things falling
from black trees.

Are they petals, leaves or birds?
They cannot be the cabbage whites
he batted briefly with his paws,
or the puffball seeds in summer grass.

They make no sound, they have no wings
and yet they can whirl and fly around
until they swoop like swallows, and
disappear into the ground.

"Where do they go?" he questions,
with eyes ablaze, following their flight
into black stone. So I put him
out into the yard, to make their acquaintance.

He has to look up at them: when one
blanches his coral nose, he sneezes,
and flicks a few from his whiskers, from
his sharpened ear, that picks up silences.

He catches one on a curled-up paw
and licks it quickly, before
its strange milk fades, then sniffs its ghost,
a wetness, while his black coat

shivers with stars of flickering frost.
—And with something else that makes his thin
tail swish, his fur stand on end!
Then he suddenly scoots in

and sits again with wide eyes
at the firelit window, sees
white things falling
from black trees.

James Kirkup

WINTER TRYST

Love's delight
On a frosty night
Shines brighter for
The dark trees whispering
Sedition around the house
And the fire within.

Open the door to the wind:
The word sin
Is a delicious tempter
As the cat steps in
With his lopsided grin.

He knows we know
He knows. His yellow eyes
Glow. He's wise. So,
While the winds blow,

Now comes the hour
In which we must devour
Us, time, and light.
Out, night.
            In, cat. Don't go.
We need you here, for though

We, in heedless flight,
Blow out each spark
Along love's leaping arc
Of fire, and all is dark
To sight, your eyes will light
Our way home through the night.

Ormonde de Kay, Jr.

THE KITTEN AND FALLING LEAVES

See the Kitten on the wall,
Sporting with the leaves that fall,
Withered leaves—one-two-and three—
From the lofty elder-tree!
Through the calm and frosty air
Of this morning bright and fair,
Eddying round and round they sink
Softly, slowly: one might think,
From the motions that they made,
Every little leaf conveyed
Sylph or Faery hither tending,
To this lower world descending,
Each invisible and mute
In his wavering parachute.

—But the Kitten, how she starts,
Crouches, stretches, paws, and darts!
First at one, and then its fellow
Just as light and just as yellow.
There are many now—now one—
Now they stop and there are none:
What intenseness of desire
In her upward eye of fire!
With a tiger-leap half-way

Now she meets the coming prey,
Lets it go as fast, and then
Has it in her power again:
Now she works with three or four,
Like an Indian conjurer;
Quick as he in feats of art,
Far beyond in joy of heart.
Were her antics played in the eye
Of a thousand standers-by,
Clapping hands with shout and stare,
What would little Tabby care
For the plaudits of the crowd!

William Wordsworth

A DOMESTIC CAT

The cat I live with is an animal
Conceived as I, though next to me she's small.
More like each other, so our births assert,
Than either one is like a house or shirt.
I nervous at my table,
She by the stove and stable,
Show what a gap lies between cats and men;
But shift the point of view to see again
Surrounding both of us disgusting death,
Death frames us then in this still room, each pumping breath.

Her white fur where she cleaneth it smells like talc;
Her claws can tap the floor in a rapid walk,
Her shape in walking bulges up and down;
Jealous, she sits remote, but does not frown.
To sleep, she puts an eye

Upside down next a thigh
And lost the small snout grows a deeper pink;
To eat, above the neck her elbows shrink,
The outstretched neck, the head tilt when she chews,
They thrust, they gulp, and sated she rises to refuse.

Compelled, as men by God are, twice each year
Her look turned stony, she will disappear;
Exhausted, three days later, dirty and plain
She will creep home, and be herself again.
She cleans her young contented,
At one month they're presented,
Clear-eyed she hauls them out and on my bed;
Here, while they wolf her tits, she purrs, outspread.
She waves her tail, they look, they leap, they riot,
She talks. And later, when they've gone, she cowers quiet.

Graceful as the whole sky, which time goes through,
Through going time she wanders, graceful too.
Sits in the sun, sleeps rounded on a chair,
Answers my voicc with a green limpid stare.
Modest in drooping furs
She folds her paws and purrs
Charmed by the curious song of friendly talk;
But hearing up the stair a stamping walk,
Under the bed she streaks, weakly disgraced,
As humble as an alleycat that's being chased.

We live through time. I'll finish with a dream:
Wishing to play and bored, so she did seem;
But said, she knew two kittens just outside
That she could play with any time she tried;
We went to see this thing,
But one hung by a string,
A kitten strung up high, and that looked dead;
But when I took it down, it was well instead.
All three then played and had a pleasant time.
So at war dreamt a soldier for him I made this rhyme.

Edwin Denby

THE INNKEEPER'S CAT

The cat climbed into blazing night
along the palm's elliptic stem,
a speck in overwhelming light,
to prowl the roofs of Bethlehem.

Midnight was chill, so he crawled back
by the inn stable where he knew
warm creatures slept, but through a crack
strange radiance made him pause and mew.

A man as splendid as a king
opened the door and let him in;
he saw the gold and heard them sing,
his fur got prickly on his skin.

He could not hum the hymns he heard,
nor mumble prayers, but in caress,
he tiptoed to the Child and purred,
and rubbed against His Mother's dress.

Ulrich Troubetzkoy

TO A CAT

Cat! who has pass'd thy grand climacteric,
How many mice and rats hast in thy days
Destroy'd?—How many titbits stolen? Gaze
With those bright languid segments green, and prick
Those velvet ears—but prithee do not stick
Thy latent talons in me—and upraise
Thy gentle mew—and tell me all thy frays
Of fish and mice, and rats and tender chick.

Nay, look not down, nor lick thy dainty wrists—
For all the wheezy asthma—and for all
Thy tail's tip is nick'd off—and though the fists
Of many a maid have given thee many a maul,
Still is that fur as soft as when the lists
In youth thou enter'dst on glass-bottled wall.

John Keats

CATS

Cats sleep
Anywhere,
Any table,
Any chair,
Top of piano,
Window-ledge,
In the middle,
On the edge,
Open drawer,
Empty shoe,
Anybody's
Lap will do,
Fitted in a
Cardboard box,
In the cupboard
With your frocks—
Anywhere!
They don't care!
Cats sleep
Anywhere.

Eleanor Farjeon

COMFORT

As I mused by the hearthside,
Puss said to me:
"There burns the fire, man,
And here sit we

"Four Walls around us
Against the cold air;
And the latchet drawn close
To the draughty Stair.

"A Roof o'er our heads
Star-proof, moon-immune,
And a wind in the chimney
To wait us a tune.

"What Felicity!" miaowed he,
"Where none may intrude;
Just Man and Beast—met
In this Solitude!

"Dear God, what security,
Comfort and bliss!
And to think, too, what ages
Have brought us to this!

"You in your sheeps-wool coat,
Buttons of bone,
And me in my fur-about
On the warm hearthstone."

Walter de la Mare

THE DEATH OF A CAT

I

Since then, those months ago, these rooms miss something,
A link, a spark, and the street down there reproves
My negligence, particularly the gap
For the new block which, though the pile of timber
Is cleared on which he was laid to die, remains
A gap, a catch in the throat, a missing number.

You were away when I lost him, he had been absent
Six nights, two dead, which I had not learnt until
You returned and asked and found how he had come back
To a closed door having scoured the void of Athens
For who knows what and at length, more than unwell
Came back and less than himself, his life in tatters.

Since when I dislike that gap in the street and that obdurate
Dumb door of iron and glass and I resent
This bland blank room like a doctor's consulting room
With its too many exits, all of glass and frosted,
Through which he lurked and fizzed, a warm retort,
Found room for his bag of capers, his bubbling flasket.

For he was our puck, our miniature lar, he fluttered
Our dovecot of visiting cards, he flicked them askew,
The joker among them who made a full house. As you said,
He was a fine cat. Though how strange to have, as you said later,
Such a personal sense of loss. And looking aside
You said, but unconvincingly: What does it matter?

II

To begin with he was a beautiful object:
Blue crisp fur with a white collar,
Paws of white velvet, springs of steel,
A Pharaoh's profile, a Krishna's grace,
Tail like a questionmark as a masthead

And eyes dug out of a mine, not the dark
Clouded tarns of a dog's, but cat's eyes—
Light in a rock crystal, light distilled
Before his time and ours, before cats were tame.

To continue, he was alive and young,
A dancer, incurably male, a clown,
With his gags, his mudras, his entrechats,
His triple bends and his double takes.
Firm as a Rameses in African wonderstone,
Fluid as Krishna chasing the milkmaids,
Who hid under carpets and nibbled at olives,
Attacker of ankles, nonesuch of nonsense,
Indolent, impudent, cat catalytic.

* * *

To continue further: if not a person
More than a cipher, if not affectionate
More than indifferent, if not volitive
More than automaton, if not self-conscious
More than mere conscious, if not useful
More than a parasite, if allegorical
More than heraldic, if man-conditioned
More than a gadget, if perhaps a symbol
More than a symbol, if somewhat a proxy
More than a stand-in—was what he was!
A self-contained life, was what he must be
And is not now: more than an object.

And is not now. Spreadeagled on coverlets—
Those are the coverlets, bouncing on chairbacks—
These are the chairs, pirouetting and sidestepping,
Feinting and jabbing, breaking a picture frame—
Here is the picture, tartar and sybarite,
One minute quicksilver, next minute butterballs,
Precise as a fencer, lax as an odalisque,
And in his eyes the light from the mines
One minute flickering, steady the next,

Lulled to a glow or blown to a blaze,
But always the light that was locked in the stone
Before his time and ours; at best semi-precious
All stones of that kind yet, if not precious,
Are more than stones, beautiful objects
But more than objects. While there is light in them.

III

Canyons of angry sound, catastrophe, cataclysm,
Smells and sounds in cataracts, cat-Athens,
Not, not the Athens we know, each whisker buzzing
Like a whole Radar station, typhoons of grapeshot,
Crossfire from every roof of ultra-violet arrows
And in every gutter landmines, infra-red,
A massed barrage of too many things unknown
On too many too quick senses (cossetted senses
Of one as spoilt as Pangur Ban, Old Foss
Or My Cat Jeoffrey), all the drab and daily
Things to him deadly, all the blunt things sharp,
The paving stones a sword dance. Chanting hawkers
Whose street cries consecrate their loaves and fishes
And huge black chessmen carved out of old priests
And steatopygous boys, they all were Gogs and Magogs
With seven-league battering boots and hair-on-ending voices
Through which he had to dodge. And all the wheels
Of all the jeeps, trucks, trams, motor-bicycles, buses, sports cars,
Caught in his brain and ravelled out his being
To one high horrible twang of breaking catgut,
A swastika of lightning. Such was Athens
To this one indoors cat, searching for what
He could not grasp through what he could not bear,
Dragged to and fro by unseen breakers, broken
At last by something sudden; then dragged back
By his own obstinate instinct, a long dark thread
Like Ariadne's ball of wool in the labyrinth
Not now what he had played with as a kitten

But spun from his own catsoul, which he followed
Now that the minotaur of machines and men
Had gored him, followed it slowly, slowly, until
It snapped a few yards short of a closed door,
Of home, and he lay on his side like a fish on the pavement
While the ball of wool rolled back and down the hill,
His purpose gone, only his pain remaining
Which, even if purpose is too human a word
Was not too human a pain for a dying cat.

IV

Out of proportion? Why, almost certainly,
You and I, darling, knew no better
Than to feel worse for it. As one feels worse
When a tree is cut down, an ear-ring lost,
A week-end ended, a child at nurse
Weaned. Which are also out of proportion.

Sentimentality? Yes, it is possible;
You and I, darling, are not above knowing
The tears of the semi-, less precious things,
A pathetic fallacy perhaps, as the man
Who gave his marble victory wings
Was the dupe—who knows—of sentimentality.

Not really classic. The Greek Anthology
Laments its pets (like you and me, darling),
Even its grasshoppers; dead dogs bark
On the roads of Hades where poets hang
Their tiny lanterns to ease the dark.
Those poets were late though. Not really classical.

Yet more than an object? Why, most certainly.
You and I, darling, know that sonatas
Are more than sound and that green grass
Is more than grass or green, which is why
Each of our moments as they pass
Is of some moment; more than an object.

So this is an epitaph, not for calamitous
Loss but for loss; this was a person
In a small way who had touched our lives
With a whisk of delight, like a snatch of a tune
From which one whole day's mood derives.
For you and me, darling, this is an epitaph.

Louis MacNeice

VIGNETTE OF SUMMER

On the cool thick grass under a sycamore
Is poured Mr. Jingle, the cat, a pool of blackness
So strong he seems to suck all shadow in,
Himself the essence of surrounding shade.
Egypt is in the crook of his straight tail,
The small carved bony triangle of face
Drawn out in nubian profile, immobile
As any Pharoah's. I'll not try
To guess his dreams, except he breathes out bliss
In sweet and regular cadence, sleep distilled,
To delicately steam the air above him,
Mingling with breath of wild white roses, clover,
Bay, gorse, wild broom. The leaf-bruised air of summer
Is honey-thick above his slumbering head,
While close beside, a shaft of sun on grass
Gives him a hump of emerald on his back.
The scene is struck like a new-minted coin
Upon the mind; of many such small hoards
Whole seasons reconstruct; joy's random gold
Built up of such inconsequential scenes,
Oddly and inappropriately to bring, in cold

And sodden seasons, the scent of wild white rose,
And in a closed and sunless winter room
Summer's spreading green stain.

Frances Minturn Howard

IF BLACK

I have a cat, and if black is apropos,
an eternal no—
except for his round gold eyes that greenishly glow
and the fleet way he plays,
leaping to toss whatever it is with his paws

while those needles of white flick at the ends of his toes.
He's a quickness that flows
more than it runs, a dainty panther of poise
as he noiselessly goes
night black from the tip of his tail to his nose.

In some ways a simile cat, but unlike those
snarling obscene
black cats arched for evil's Halloween
or told of by Poe
he's not so much metaphor dark as a lightfooted show,

a living example of just how wrong we can be
when we think we see
bad luck when we don't, and that we lack
perception, in fact,
when we call a cat something else because it is black.

Harold Witt

DEATH OF THE BLACK CAT, MR. JINGLE

I will not say you moved among us shade,
But that, if shadow made itself a shape,
It would, I think, be yours.

A movement just beyond the eye's small province
Infers a presence now denied to sight.
It ripples smoothly over ankle-bone,
Arches against the knee. If I could touch
What moves outside all searching, it would be
Familiar to me, though it still elude
My conscious vision, hooding golden eyes.

String on a chain the small absurdities
We say farewell to, dying with their creature—
We, frozen in bleak immortality
Who bury one by one our little loves.
Is grace the less because it's very small?
Must elegance assume a certain scale,
Or can it flow like water on a wall?

When he with the lightest gesture flicked a beetle
From the mantle-shelf, it was a royal dismissal
Conjuring princes and their embroidered kerchiefs.
Silence, in him, took tangible dimension—
He moved in ordered triangles of space,
And all his lines flowed long and angular
Into stark hieroglyphs of pure distinction.

And too, he had that extra quality
Of rareness, that insane dimension
Of the unpredictable. He, most decorous prince,
Became afire with greed at the smell of a clam—
Or suddenly, inappropriately affectionate,
Would leap the room to blow up a snowstorm of papers,
Having acquired a taste for demonstrative love.

Where has he gone? Is there room for fur in heaven?
If cloudy angels spread their vapourous wings

In a great void, nothing beneath the hand
To warm it into life, I don't want heaven.
It is the small particulars that build
The citadels of our identity,
And mine is dwindled by his vanished shade.

Frances Minturn Howard

CHARADE

For more than two years now
he's known
that we're the lonely ones
this Siamese and I.

I toss the knotted string
he plays the clown
leaping in graceful arcs and turns
pursuing bits of lifeless twine
to please me, while

he dreams of chasing butterflies thru fields . . .
his nose uplifted to the scented wind
remembers rabbits that gave chase, and mice,
and one small bird that came
within his grasp.

Only the sapphire eyes, off-guard,
suggest the secret
frozen in twin blue pools
that have looked upon betrayal.

Declawed, ungendered, royal line at end
sentenced to life alone, indoors,
but loving still

he winds around my leg and purrs
apology
for his dream
and dedicates his sorrow
to the one
who has no dream at all.

Aline Beveridge

ONE FOR A GUY WHO WAS A CAT

He is the ground's thing now
Who was its stroller and its viewer,
The harrier of all that flew, crawled, moved
Beneath his near-sighted nose.
A rose in the garden was his Nameless,
Or a cloud in the sky for pausing under,
Or to paw; its thorns bit his thighs pleasantly.
Under ground rules now, he is the crawled-upon,
Who once loafed at large over Maytime grass,
Or leisured long autumnal afternoons
In the peace of direct sunlight,
As much at ease with the growth
And the decline of seasons, as with his own skin.
One of all round earth's things that grow and decline,
Age stroked him with an unkind hand,
And broke his beauty and his simple power
Of learning ground's lore;
He is the garden corner's Nameless now,
Where he is folded lovingly in the ground's book
Like its pressed flower.

Nancy G. Westerfield

TWO SICK KITTENS

The two sick kittens, round-eyed, stare
As if I were the one to be tamed
Or give them what they ask by being there.
Nothing between us can be really claimed,
But I, as nurse, can touch the heavy head
With what should be a tongue but is a hand,
And all night long they purr upon my bed,
Their presence there at all like a command.
Who can resist the sad animal gaze
That takes us in, so close always to fear,
So close to pain, where violence obeys
That deeper instinct that would have us hear,
And pays the price—for what? For human love?
Whatever they implore that we must give.

May Sarton

MARMALADE LOST

Her honey fur pointed down her back
to her almost lady hips.

She only showed her claws for love,
was particular about her paws,

and never first to dinner.
Hated rain, liked beds,

was clever climbing down a tree,
the hardest part for kittens.

Did a yen for wandering tempt her,
lured by a hedge or a tom?

Did a truck betray her?
For ten days I've prayed her home,

running like a little bell at dusk,
bouncing like a ballerina,

dainty at my opening door.

Ruth Whitman

THE CAT NAMED COLETTE

She was spidery, a flower-small kitten;
creature of angles and tangents.
Whims formed her decisions.
She danced on a web of her making,
conjuring, conquering victims.
Like spiked leaf or pointed blossom,
she lived mid-air.

She is now, curved petal on petal,
an enormous peony:
the actress pleased with herself,
perfecting rites of indolence,
performing the role of her roundness.
She wears, always, white furs
whose dense folds are golden.

She keeps the delicate chin of her namesake,
the thin Sphinx smile.
Her intense, theatrical gaze,
beaming from black-ringed eyes,
is rich with self-love.

Joanne de Longchamps

IN WINTER

Having woken, with two cats
on the bed, half-risen rubbed my
eyes, reached out and touched
one, was it one
head or two, I stirred,
shook, and was wide awake. One purred,
stretched,
yawning, as I turned:
one lay encurled
in sleep still. As in Egypt,
or in Siam,
on some lost morning, a wind
settled, so now
the darkness eased
into soft breathing where four mouths
opened to the sun. I drank light
through my nose, as they did,
as she did, humped beside me
waiting for the full blaze. When it came,
striking through the windows
as with a plough-share, the rivensoil
of the room
gave birth. With a cry,
one stepped
to the ground. One leapt,
washing itself,
to the sill. Dreaming,
I turned again and slept, as she did,
as they did, remembering
all that had happened, and what
was still to come.

George MacBeth

VAGABOND PRINCE

He came to us shadow-flat
But nevertheless a Cat
Spelled with a capital C,
And—we being what we were—
He's now the vast hauteur
Or ruffed rotundity.

A crisp, imperious mew,
When dinner, overdue,
Delays upon the shelf,
Reminds us of the need,
The privilege, indeed,
Of waiting on Himself.

Both cream-fed pillow-sleeper
And gaunt-ribbed alley-creeper
Who lacks an ear and eye
Could give a rajah lessons
How to confer his presence
On mere humanity.

Anne Barlow

KITTEN

The tiny creature, fawn and white,
That late exchanged womb—dark for light
And cannot quite believe the air
Is something for a cat to tear
Like paper and yet not be torn,
Wearied now of being born

Knows, between your arm and breast,
Reasonless, rewarding rest,
Safe in wonder, safe in love
From what cats are fearful of.
I, who am too long alive
Thriving as the ruthless thrive
Have, between your breast and arm
Found an equal pity warm—
Safe in love and safe in wonder
From the storm men cower under,
Storm of wind-blown passion's raging,
Storm of fear and storm of aging—
Pity pure as water-shine
Melting all flesh—heavy mine,
Or flesh that romps as kittens do
Certain of recourse to you.

Raymond Holden

COMMUNICATION

Whether resenting the personal insult of rain,
upstaging her perennial enemy, the dog,
or cuffing the nonsense out of an explosion of kittens,
my unflappable cat
speaks more eloquently than many
an over-diploma'd diplomat.

Jennie M. Palen

LOOKING FOR ITSY

2 A.M.—the hour of rats
racing across alleys, junk
heaving in its graveyards, the hour
of strained bones like nerves whining
inside their shells of flesh.
2 A.M.—the dark hides nothing
but a lost cat, nothing but her whimper
as she runs to hide from the scarecrow
buildings, the rotten windows,
and the automobile parts
thrown into the block-wide lot.

Into the desert we come, breathing hard,
the search party fanning out through the weeds
and the broken glass.
                    There is no time
for panic, we must find her. She is lost
and alone in this metal jungle, the back yard
of nowhere. We are three shadows
bent over to see what the ash cans hide,
pale under our hearts,
listening between heartbeats.

We step into a darker nightmare
as if from one hell down to another,
a dead cat screaming silently
lying at our feet. What's left is gray and white;
gray and white becomes the color of our dread.
A dead cat frozen in the moonlight.

She is somewhere
in this hell of rubble
where rats are boatmen
beating on metal rivers.
She is somewhere
among this spiky junk,
an animal at bay

in a final thicket
where no leaves fall.

All night long we call her
up and down the alleys,
scared of the slithering rats
and the black doorways.
With hope gone like a candle
at the end of night,
we call her and call her:
"Itsy! Itsy! Itsy!"

And take a vow in the milky light
of clouds turning pink with sunrise
to help every creature lost on the highways,
in the darkest sides of the city,
wherever there is no quarter.
And ask nothing in return,
only the chance of Itsy found again.
We take the vow of helpfulness.

Then like an answer we hear her calling
and see her perched on a pile of junk,
crying her dismay, so far from her own tree,
her kittens and her tuna fish.
We take her up and carry her, off
into the morning, grown soft, and home.

Naomi Lazard

PROCESSION

Stiller than zeros of silence Cat comes in,
with minus quantities of quiet, spun
in a nought of attic on some nulling loom.
His yardages of hush in our loud room

he's wearing: sovereign cape from tongue to tail.
Pervasive plush, it nudges us and we kneel
to lift the hem from rubbing our clumsy shoe.
We clear the royal passage. The least we can do .

Norma Farber

DECEMBER CATS

Less and less they walk the wild
Cold world of dark, of windy snow.
Curiosity comes in;
There is nothing more to know;
Examines corners; yawns and dies,
Warm under lamps and buzzing flies.

The oldest beast, with panther head,
The latest yielded: ran in tracks
Himself had punctured; hid by stones
And pounced, and crackled mice's backs.
But now that all midwinter wests,
Even he the ranger rests.

Mark Van Doren

CATALOG

Cats sleep fat and walk thin.
Cats, when they sleep, slump;
When they wake, pull in—
And where the plump's been
There's skin.
Cats walk thin.

Cats wait in a lump,
Jump in a streak.
Cats, when they jump, are sleek
As a grape slipping its skin—
They have technique.
Oh, cats don't creak.
They sneak.

Cats sleep fat.
They spread comfort beneath them
Like a good mat,
As if they picked the place
And then sat.
You walk around one
As if he were the City Hall
After that.

If male,
A cat is apt to sing upon a major scale:
This concert is for everybody, this
Is wholesale.
For a baton, he wields a tail.

(He is also found,
When happy, to resound
With an enclosed and private sound.)

A cat condenses.
He pulls in his tail to go under bridges,
And himself to go under fences.
Cats fit
In any size box or kit;
And if a large pumpkin grew under one,
He could arch over it.

When everyone else is just ready to go out,
The cat is just ready to come in.
He's not where he's been.
Cats sleep fat and walk thin.

Rosalie Moore

POLKA DOT

is more than cat
inviolate feline personality
with progeny for proof
white and tawny
a kind of calico cat
darkened to a trace of sherry
in an afternoon glass
quietly dusting her nose
in red petunias
she looks to the window
if I call 'hey cat'
walks with ginger steps
to sit beside her outside dish
where sun dials away the summer

like dill in season
eyes soft as early amber
shine and cover daylight

waiting for tuna
waiting for her kittens
that from the roundness of her
could arrive at any minute
she licks mittened paws
sniffs a broken rose
leaps to a monarch butterfly
strayed from a lost migration
and finally gazes with longing
at cardinals in the tree
she will not climb

David Locher

THE ARTIST SKETCHES ONE CAT

Trace
the
cat
(if you can),

Trace
one
leg
thrust
out
into space
and
darting red tongue,

Trace
whiskers
catching the sun,
spelling their length.

Trace
one
paw
curled and
swiping at an
invisible piece of
something on the carpet.

Trace
sudden turn,
stomach up,
stretch of front paws
and
sleepy.

Elizabeth Yungul

THE DEATH OF THE KITCHEN CAT

He knew his place: not to nose past
The curve of yellow counters, not to walk
Upon the soft carpets, not to appraise
The bric-a-breakables, and to stay
Closest to the alley, his properest habitat.
At the door when he panhandled, he abased himself:
Entered only sideways, and went around the room
Against its walls, watching the faces
And utensils cannily, for any sudden manna.
Self-effacing even in his last extremity,
When the alley had delivered him to death-blows,
He spoke Hello at the door almost
With his usual jaunty, and getting in
Lay flat against the wall, hunching his legs
Together out of any passer's way.
And while the meal's preparation went ahead
That would not include him, he let us see
How breakable a small thing is,
How white is death, how tidy can be kept
A kitchen corner where only the humblest
Takes his final breath.

Nancy G. Westerfield

IF CATS DON'T GO TO HEAVEN, WHAT WILL THE ANGELS STRING THEIR HARPS WITH?

1.

For the happy concept embodied in my title
I am indebted, most immediately, to Arthur Godfrey.
Beyond that, I suppose he would be the first to admit
That he did not invent it:
Something he heard, or that someone sent him.

Myself, I give him credit for passing it on
To more people simultaneously
Than any other theologian.

2.

To mew,
Or to appeal plaintively for entrance
When the door appears closed—

To purr,
Or to express gratitude
For mercy expected or unexpected—

To miaow,
As from hunger—

To caterwaul,
As in love,
Or when the moon shines down on the backs of a row of houses
Inhabited by neighbors,
Human families
More or less acquainted—

To snarl and rage,
In combat, in male rivalry—

After death, to be thrown
In sportive contempt
Upon a stage where a bad actor
Has achieved a role too sumptuous for his talents:

These are feline traits.
It is customary to distinguish
Animals which have souls from those with none.

3.

When I die
(And it is a feat no man needs to blush for)
I should like to take with me
A cat or two,
For company in the intervals between testimony.

Myron H. Broomell

2.

DEMONIC

BLACK CAT

Glances even at an apparition
still seem somehow to reverberate;
here on this black fell, though, the emission
of your strongest gaze will dissipate:

as a maniac, precipitated
into the surrounding black, will be
halted headlong and evaporated
by his padded cell's absorbency.

All the glances she was ever swept with
on herself she seems to be concealing
where, with lowering and peevish mind they're
being downlooked upon her and slept with.
As if wakened, though, she turns her face
full upon your own quite suddenly,
and in the yellow amber of those sealing
eyes of hers you unexpectedly
meet the glance you've given her, enshrined there
like an insect of some vanished race.

Rainer Maria Rilke

CAT

The fat cat on the mat
    may seem to dream
of nice mice that suffice
    for him, or cream;
but he free, maybe,
    walks in thought
unbowed, proud, where loud
    roared and fought

his kin, lean and slim,
      or deep in den
in the East feasted on beasts
      and tender men.

The giant lion with iron
      claw in paw,
and huge ruthless tooth
      in gory jaw;
the pard dark-starred,
      fleet upon feet,
that oft soft from aloft
      leaps on his meat
where woods loom in gloom—
      far now they be,
      fierce and free,
      and tamed as he;
but fat cat on the mat
      kept as a pet,
      he does not forget.

J. R. R. Tolkien

THE BIRD FANCIER

Up to his shoulders
In grasses coarse as silk,
The white cat with the yellow eyes
Sits with his paws together,
Tall as a quart of milk.

He hardly moves his head
To touch with neat nose

What his wary whiskers tell him
Is here a weed
And here a rose.

His sleepy eyes are wild with birds.
Every sparrow, thrush, and wren
Widens their furred horizons;
Then their flying song
Narrows them again.

James Kirkup

REMEMBERED CAT

Through the long orchard of a childhood dream,
under the blossom-loaded branches of the cherry,
the hunting cat moves with a rippling gleam,
parting the grass with muscled shoulders, rippled and furry.
Green gore to golden eye, love shadowy and late
under the hot frost of that glancing look—
this is the cat that will crouch and spring, and sate
the tendoned breast in him, and then at my gate
will yowl with murmured penitence. I at my book
will hear and let him in. Then, later, curling
at window ledge, the wise smile cupping the jowl,
he will murmur his sly love, letting hate
sink down with embered glow through memory's gate,
knowing the moon will return with freedom, with howl
of fighters over the wild grass, and soft sound purling
under the shadowy vines where the lovers wait.

Through all the winding years of childhood moves
this tawny cat I loved and watched, and fed,

and heard above the sound of sleet and snow,
prowling the world, while I lay warm in bed.
No night is dark, no swollen wind of autumn blows
without my hearing, far, and sad, and wild—
yet filled with all my longings too—that cry
horrid and bestial, murmured, and loving, and mild;
and yet I knew, I knew though still a child
that under the shadowy gold of the fur there glowed
the lava and the molten force of worlds
that lived at time's beginning curved my sky
with sunburst, made the heart throb in the necks of girls,
and drove me through a world of beauty hungrily.

Gold cat immortal parting the dew-bright grass,
crossing the windy orchards of years, hot life in your eye,
thanks for the furtive friendship, the hours of youth,
when under your savage voice sang the music of truth,
when the urge of beast for love lay under the glass
of your green-gold watching. Even as I,
you knew the fight, the claw, the smell of blood.
Thanks for that lesson—that beauty molder in motion
and locking the hunger of flesh with the earth and the ocean
and all things lonely and lost under mortal sky.

George Abbe

THE THING ABOUT CATS

Cats hang out with witches quite a lot;
that's not it.

The thing about cats is
they're always looking at you.
Especially when you're asleep.

Some cats pretend they're not looking
until you're not looking.
They are not to be trusted.

Some cats scowl because they're wearing
imitation fur. They feel inferior.

Some other cats look at you straight on
so that you can't drink your drink
or make love
                    but keep thinking
that cat's looking at me straight on.

But all cats do the same:
they look at you
                         and you look out
and in.

A cat is not a conscience; I'm not
saying that.
What I'm saying is
                            why are they looking?

John L'Heureux

AH HOW MY CAT BENJAMIN

Ah how my cat Benjamin flies this midnight
At the window glass, and droops his yellow length along the sill,
Moaning for the cat-cobbled streets and slit-lit lamps
Of his long half grown dreams. All shadows move
Beyond the glass, and mysteries of noise and smells unravel
Before dun sooted bodies hot hearted stalking still.

How I do desire in my glass room heavy at his shoulder
To unglass us both, were not my powers less than his,
And spin us darkly tumbling to reproach the dogs
Amid stretching streets; and light green slant-eyed candles
In every darkened door and lair to enmity or love,
Till in a biding patient day, we lick real wounds in an open place.

Pauline M. Leet

DR. FAUSTUS TO HIS CAT

Ah, stay, Grimalkin, flatter me to my doom;
Steal like a shadow in this somber room,
Enrich its fateful silence with thy purr,
Spurn not my restless hand upon thy fur
Dowered with youth for which I, fool, once gave
My all in all. Thou goest bright and brave
Locked, whiskered, at an age would turn to ashes
The golden curls of Helen; thine eye flashes
Like a lanthorn still; gay is thy sport
If grandson or if grandsire pay thee court.

Malkin, we serve one master, blackavised,
The Prince of Darkness. Oft have I surmised
Why the All-loving spake to thee in ire:
"Go seek a nook beside the quenchless fire,
Nor pray a shelter in the Heavenly house."
Did He behold thy way with bird or mouse
Trembling between thy paws? But thou didst sin
After thy nature only, I within
My sacred soul, and thus eternity
Measures my doom, while one far day may see
Thee sated with Hell creep home a prodigal

To the Father's feet, and there thy prey let fall
Unscathed, a wistful prayer in thy soft miaou
To win His smile of welcome. Even now
Satan adores thee whom he cannot hold
While me scorns safe pent within his fold.
So variously, Grimalkin, we are undone:
Thy portion cream, mine nightshade, of the Evil One.

Anne Young

THE PRIZE CAT

Pure blood domestic, guaranteed,
Soft-mannered, musical in purr,
The ribbon had declared the breed,
Gentility was in the fur.

Such feline culture in the gads
No anger ever arched her back—
What distance since those velvet pads
Departed from the leopard's track!

And when I mused how Time had thinned
The jungle strains within the cells,
How human hands had disciplined
Those prowling optic parallels;

I saw the generations pass
Along the reflex of a spring,
A bird had rustled in the grass,
The tab had caught it on its wing:

Behind the leap so furtive-wild
Was such ignition in the gleam,
I thought an Abyssinian child
Had cried out in the whitethroat's scream.

E. J. Pratt

CAT FROM THE NIGHT

All night a branch of the cypress tree
Knocked on the pane till I broke it free
To thump to the ground. In a moment a scratch
Harried the door. I lifted the latch,
And a cat rushed in like death's dark wind.
He was blacker than crow-wings; his middle was thinned
To fear and hunger. Everywhere
I stepped he stepped, with his green-lit stare
And his pleading purr, till I fed him cream
While the wind in the tree was a witch-wailed scream.

Nights now, curled snug in the hearth fire's bliss,
At a sound outside he will rise and hiss
With his back thrust high and his fur thrust higher
As he glares at the window with midnight ire.
And often by day in his windowed niche
His body will quiver, his tail will twitch,
As he stares at the bent, scarred cypress tree
And nothing else—that I can see.

Hortense Roberta Roberts

THE DRUNKARD TO HIS GELDED CAT

Scat! You stinking prune-nutted cadger. Scat!
Go claw some unsuspecting rodent
For your meal, you dud, you nuck, you cat!
I am too fried to even stew a linnet.

Go swish your tail into a wall plug,
Mendicant mumper, solicitous scab!
Go tell your sad tale to the rug,
Petitional pothunter, supplicant tab!

Demonic

You cannot charm me from this chair,
You impotent, testicless tom,
So hide in your secret ball of hair,
For tomorrow the hangover comes!

Paul Zimmer

THE RATLESS CAT

When I came home my mother cat said,
"Tom," she said, "I wish I was dead."
When I came home my father cat bawled,
"It's cats like you make it tough for us all!"
When I came home my brother cat scratched me
And said he wished a dog would catch me.
When I came home my sister cat said,
"You put the gray hairs on mama cat's head."
When I came home my grandpa cat spat,
"You ruined the last years of a feeble old cat!"

When I came home without a rat,
Mom, pop, brother, sis, and grandpa cat
Took one long look, gave one loud groan,
When I came home, when I came home.

Naomi Replansky

LINES FOR A FAVORITE CAT

Escaping for twelve years
The nearly always imminent deaths,
My wary and beautiful cat
Pawtucket
Died last night
In the teeth of a masked
And murderous coon,
Loudly caterwauling his rage and terror
At the full moon
As she turned away
Her blandly betraying bitch-face
From the floodlit death arena.

Good-bye,
Roller of bobbins, balls, dice,
Devilish feather-strewer!
Old three-striker at gopher holes.
Good-bye.

This is the way things are:
I have carried your bedding of ferns
To the deep hole I have dug, crossed
Your paws in the way
You used to sleep.
This is the way life is,
And I must make do, somehow,
Without you.

Even making a pet, perhaps, of your enemy
The coon, who has cleaned your dish
And is already picking the lock
Of the back door
With dexterous and beseeching hands.

Eric Barker

THE CAT

They call me cruel. Do I know if mouse or
songbird feels?
I only know they make me light and salutary meals:
And if, as 'tis my nature to, ere I devour I tease 'em,
Why should a low-bred gardener's boy pursue me
with a besom?

C. S. Calverly

O CAT OF CARLISH KIND

That vengeance I ask and cry,
By way of exclamation,
On all the whole cat nation
Of cattes wild and tame:
God send them sorrow and shame!
That cat specially
That slew so cruelly
My litell pretty sparrow
That I brought up at Carow.
O cat of carlish kind,
The finde was in thy mind
Whan thou my bird untwined!
I would thou haddest ben blind!
The leopards savage,
The lions in their rage,
Might catch thee in their paws,
And gnaw thee in their jaws!
The serpentes of Lybany
Might stinge thee venimously!

The dragons with their tongues
Might poison thy liver and lungs!
The manticors of the mountains
Might feed them on thy brains! . . .
Of Inde the greedy gripes
Might tear out all thy tripes!
Of Arcady the bears
Might pluck away thine ears!
The wild wolf Lycaon
Bite asunder thy back bone!
Of Ethna the brenning hill,
That day and night brenneth still,
Set in thy tail a blaze,
That all the world may gaze
And wonder upon thee,
From Ocean the great sea
Unto the Isles of Orchady,
From Tillbery ferry
To the plain of Salisbery!
So traitorously my bird to kill
That never ought thee evil will! . . .

John Skelton

INDOOR JUNGLE BLUES

Across the deep-piled jungle of our rooms,
he prowls the Persian patterns like a veldt
and winds his way among the window blooms
weaving the leaves and light with banded pelt.

In the striped daylight of Venetian blinds
he stalks a memory of antelope
and wildebeest, but almost never finds
a mouse to nourish atavistic hope.

Alert and cunning without need to be,
he flicks his tail, crouched on the ottoman,
ears crisped to sounds that shake tranquillity—
the pouring milk, the shearing of a can.

He prowls the tropic warmth from door to door
and stares through his transparent walls of glass
at sudden gusts of birds that dart and soar
and scatter onto fountain and the grass.

Across the indoor landscape of his days
he seeks escape from cage of pampered self,
dreams wildness, closing eyes of chrysoprase,
stretched on his high dark bough—the kitchen shelf.

Ulrich Troubetzkoy

CAT-GODDESSES

A perverse habit of cat-goddesses—
Even the blackest of them, black as coals
Save for a new moon blazing on each breast,
With coral tongues and beryl eyes like lamps,
Long legged, pacing three by three in nines—
This obstinate habit is to yield themselves,
In verisimilar love-ecstasies,
To tatter-eared and slinking alley-toms
No less below the common run of cats
Than they above it; which they do for spite,
To provoke jealousy—not the least abashed
By such gross-headed, rabbit-colored litters
As soon they shall be happy to desert.

Robert Graves

THE CAT AND THE MOON

The cat went here and there
And the moon spun round like a top,
And the nearest kin of the moon,
The creeping cat, looked up.
Black Minnaloushe stared at the moon,
For, wander and wail as he would,
The pure cold light in the sky
Troubled his animal blood.
Minnaloushe runs in the grass
Lifting his delicate feet.
Do you dance, Minnaloushe, do you dance?
When two close kindred meet,
What better than call a dance:
Maybe the moon may learn,
Tired of that courtly fashion,
A new dance turn.
Minnaloushe creeps through the grass
From moonlit place to place,
The sacred moon overhead
Has taken a new phase.
Does Minnaloushe know that his pupils
Will pass from change to change,
And that from round to crescent,
From crescent to round they range?
Minnaloushe creeps through the grass
Alone, important and wise,
And lifts to the changing moon
His changing eyes.

William Butler Yeats

LOOK, SEE THE CAT

A bird's wing lies under your swing.
The cat cleans her face in a sunny place.
The mother bird screams. This is the first
lesson, but not the worst,
though a child turns cold in the sunny place
where the cat cleans her face.

Now you scream with the bird. The sleek furred
cat could never be you. Lesson two
is the long look you turn to the dark inside
places where cats hide.
Look, see the cat. This is lesson two:
the cat could be you.

Nancy Price

MOON

I have a white cat whose name is Moon
He eats catfish from a wooden spoon,
And sleeps till five each afternoon.

Moon goes out when the moon is bright
And sycamore trees are spotted white
To sit and stare in the dead of night.

Beyond still water cries a loon,
Through mulberry leaves peers a wild baboon
And in Moon's eyes I see the moon.

William Jay Smith

FIVE EYES

In Hans' old mill his three black cats
Watch his bins for the thieving rats.
Whiskers and claw, they crouch in the night,
Squeaks from the flour sacks, squeaks from where
The cold wind stirs on the empty stair,
Squeaking and scampering, everywhere.
Then down they pounce, now in, now out,
At whisking tail and sniffing snout;
While lean old Hans he snores away
Till peep of light at break of day;
Then up he climbs to his creaking mill
Out come his cats all grey with meal—
Jekkel, and Jessup, and one-eyed Jill.

Walter de la Mare

LAT TAKE A CAT

Lat take a cat, and fostre him well with milk
And tendre flesh, and make his couche of silk.
And lat him see a mous go by the wall;
Anon he weyveth milk, and flesh and al,
And every deyntee that is in the hous,
Such appetyt hath he to ete a mous.

Geoffrey Chaucer

CAT'S DREAM

How neatly a cat sleeps,
sleeps with its paws and its substance,
sleeps with its wicked claws,

and with its ruthless blood,
sleeps with all the rings—
a series of burnt circles—
which form the odd geology
of its sand-colored tail.

I should like to sleep like a cat,
with all the fur of time,
with a tongue rough as flint,
with the dry sex of fire;
and after speaking to no one,
stretch myself over the world,
over roofs and landscapes,
with a passionate desire
to hunt the rats in my dreams.

I have seen how the cat asleep
would undulate, how the night
flowed through it like dark water;
and at times, it was going to fall
or possibly plunge into
the bare deserted snowdrifts.
Sometimes it grew so much in sleep
like a tiger's great-grandfather,
and would leap in the darkness over
rooftops, clouds and volcanoes.

Sleep, sleep, cat of the night,
with episcopal ceremony
and your stone-hewn mustache.
Take care of all our dreams;
control the obscurity
of our slumbering prowess
with your relentless heart
and the great ruff of your tail.

Pablo Neruda

(*translated by* Ben Belitt
and Alastair Reid)

ON A NIGHT OF SNOW

Cat, if you go outdoors you must walk in the snow.
You will come back with little white shoes on your feet,
Little white slippers of snow that have heels of sleet.
Stay by the fire, my Cat. Lie still, do not go.
See how the flames are leaping and hissing low,
I will bring you a saucer of milk like a marguerite,
So white and so smooth, so spherical, and so sweet—
Stay with me, Cat. Out-doors the wild winds blow.

Out-doors the wild winds blow, Mistress, and dark is the night.
Strange voices cry in the trees, intoning strange lore,
And more than cats move, lit by our eyes' green light,
On silent feet where the meadow grasses hang hoar—
Mistress, there are portents abroad of magic and might,
And things that are yet to be done. Open the door!

Elizabeth J. Coatsworth

THE WIND AND THE RAIN

Today the cats are wild:
they stand upright,
and with their claws unsheathed
rake cushioned chairs;
the sofa's polished legs
have felt their spite;
they chase each other headlong
down the stairs.

Go not on a long journey,
stay indoors.
The wind is rising

and the rains will come.
The cats have summoned them:
along the floors
a coldness flows,
and thunder beats his drum.

Go not afield,
for once, stay home with me.
The fire is on the hearth,
the house is warm;
and purring, nodding, drowsing
sleepily,
the cats sit, now
that they have raised the storm.

Elizabeth J. Coatsworth

THE CAT!

Who pads through the wood
Where cypresses grow,
When the sun goes down
And the night-winds blow?
The cat!

Who slinks through the cave
In the side of the hill
Where black bats swoop
From a cobwebbed sill?
The cat!

Who purrs by the grave
Of unshriven dead,
While witches dance
And ghouls are fed?
The cat! . . SKAT! ! !

Joseph Payne Brennan

WHAT THE GRAY CAT SINGS

The Cat was once a weaver,
    A weaver, a weaver,
An old and withered weaver
    Who labored late and long;
And while she made the shuttle hum
And wove the weft and clipped the thrum,
Beside the loom with droning drum
    She sang the weaving song:
        "Pr-rrum, pr-rrum,
Thr-ree thr-reads in the thr-rum,
        Pr-rrum!"

The Cat's no more a weaver,
    A weaver, a weaver,
An old and wrinkled weaver,
    For though she did no wrong,
A witch hath changed the shape of her
That dwindled down and clothed in fur
Beside the hearth with droning purr
    She thrums her weaving song:
        "Pr-rrum, pr-rrum,
Thr-ree thr-reads in the thr-rum,
        Pr-rrum!"

Arthur Guiterman

BALLAD FOR A COAL-BLACK TOM

The coal-black cat and the chipmunk sat,
A verandah's length between them;
All stillness crouched in a feline frame,
The cat was slick as the chipmunk tame,

And never O never his yellow eyes
Betrayed his arrested energies,—
The steely limbs beneath his coat,
Desire latched from gullet to throat,—
And he stared as if his horizon were
Beyond the creature in stripèd fur.

The chipmunk sat with the coal-black cat,
A verandah's length between them;
Her deep-brown irises transfixed
And dread and decorum intermixed,
She disputed the blood in its fiery urge
As the pulse endured the arterial scourge;
Yet held her fear with assumed repose,
For never O never would she disclose
The verandah's stoven slat, where she
Preempted an open sesame,
And momentwise could escape a death
With no test word for a shibboleth.

The fabulous strength in the tiny length
Of the furred chipmunk was amazing;
Her small heart burned as her bloodstream churned,
Her glistered eyes stirred, blazing;
Her limbs recoiled as she caught a glance
Of the big tom's furious iron stance
And before his muscled and tractable paws
Held her broken neck in his blasphemous jaws,
She leaped, a current of lightning, from
The immobilized and terrible tom,
Who barricaded the unhinged slat,
Till his obstinate sleek was skeletal fat,
And he eased him through with unhurrying grace
To trouble the leaves in the hiding place.

The coal-black cat sat licking his chops,
As feline gourmets do;
With never a care he sniffed the air
And sneezed a soft *kerchoo!*

And he sniffled a sniff and cherished the whiff
And laid him down for a snooze,
As a chipmunk choir with chipmunk ire
Sang the chipmunk blues;
But the atavistic materialistic
Tom with the tigery brain
Gave a feline start as his feral heart
Set him loose on the prowl again.

I. L. Salomon

TOM PEEPER

Tom Peeper, fiery commissar
of the commune of cats in our
backyard, glares from the fire escape.
He's being punished.

An afternoon guest, today he snatched
some cheese and ran out the window. I slammed it.
Now food is being set down. There's none
for the fierce outsider.

Poor penitent, tomorrow he'll
come back, a craftier citizen
in my world perhaps. But in his own
less of a leader?

Francis Maguire

THE CAT WHOSE NAME IS MOUSE

has never seen one
but has become
a chaser of bees—
and been stung.
She is a moonlight
midnight diva
in leaping and diving
ballets-on-the-lawn,
star stalker of moths—
and she daggers them down.
Day's butterfly-leaper
captures mid-air.
Now summer's lean terror
sleeps plumply through winter.—
I imagine her dreams
are a matter of wings.

Joanne de Longchamps

CATS

They are always there: around the
Eye's corner, beneath the porch,
Slipping into some edge's shadow.

Their cautious shapes always beyond
The broom's bristles, the dog's chain.
They move in the round sense of their

Own motion, silent as thoughts.
In the white heat of the full moon
They mate like banshees; gone on

The ecstacy of their own wildness.
In the mild afternoons they stalk:
The fields, alleyways, barns are

Haunted by the quick presence of
Their predator's need. They are the
Force behind this moving surface.

Promiscuous and sleek, they flow across
Their woven world; the air charged with
Premonition and its attendant spaces.

Robert Gibb

THE CITY CATS

There's no stopping them
when they come, the city cats
who've learned to rifle, like bums,
the trash cans for fish or
chicken bones, who've learned to make it
on their own.

At night, late
in vacant lots, screams like sirens
blocks away, hideous
from apartment windows:
the tom cats tear at female fur,
yellow eyes
blank in their sex, like hunger.

Bruce H. Guernsey

THE OLD CAT

The old cat won't stay buried.
She keeps riding the rain that rhythms the roof,
or stalks the moon until dawn.
Her tongue is in the rough wind licking the trees
clean. She is dragging her bobby sock under the bed
and clawing at the grey, empty toes.

She knows, I left her under
roots of pine, nine lives stiff as cones, only fur,
and light as birds, bones. Her eyes,
now, full of bright beetles, skull vacant and dark
as an abandoned beehive, her tail flicks at the roots.
She cannot take to the earth's ancient
embrace and purrs in the thunder
that threatens to uncover
her face.

The old cat is dragging out the sock again,
bringing in dreams that won't stay buried.

Frank Finale

CAT

Today he sits majestic, a household god,
Immobile, his stare
Impassive as that Cat's for whom the
Egyptians built temples, his hair
Smooth as old onyx. . .
Yesterday, industrious, he became
Family Provider, stalked game
And, on the doorstep, offered us our share.

At other times he swaggers, insults
His peers, serenades a lady, fights
Duels—or else on nervous, windy nights
Skulks, looks black, fur blown back
Slinks in and crouches by the fire.
Asleep he twitches, in memory of witches' rites.

Come morning, he's all domesticity
Assumes a tabby air, paws clean, affectionately
Rolls over, purrs, gives
Pleasure. . . Oh this cat, this
Inhabitant of nine worlds, *lives*
Nine lives.

Ruth Graydon

STORM

Put out on the twilight porch, puss
pouts and pulls gray velvet paws
away from cold rainfingers, curling
her striped tail like anchor-rope, laws

of comfort and storm-navigation
smouldering behind green eyes—
as if she once sailed next to Noah
under identical skies.

Daisy Stieber Squadra

RETURN OF THE PRODIGAL

Where there is kindness, there the cat returns,
Black foot before black foot, with whiskers high,
Placating step, and hunger-lighted eye
That seeks the plate his whole desire burns
To fall upon. A flattened stomach yearns
For gastronomical felicity.
Where is the saucered milk that she puts by
For me alone? Ulysses here returns!
If there are cats that, shadowed by the night,
Upon this sacred spot have placed their paws
And wolfed my fish, let them look to their claws!
There will be shrieks to make the darkness bright.
For braver men than I, love being gone,
Have trotted home for food with whiskers torn.

Frances Minturn Howard

ELEGY FOR A BLACK CAT

Not mine, but I mourn him,
Si-Itam, the black cat
With a Burmese name,
Whose loud hungry cries
Roused the sleeping lovers
Before sunrise,
Whose rare rumbling purrs
Gentled dark wakeful hours.

Not mine, but I do mourn
The black cat with the wavy tail!
On pale rugs outlined

He lashed it hard
In delight or rage, who knows?
I keep his long strong whisker,
A birthday present once,
And now *Memento Mori.*

Not mine, but I mourn too
The life he shared so long,
And all such broken ends
As these departures bring,
The empty house, abandoned flowers,
And all we shared, and miss,
That was both ours and his.

Yet mourning, take comfort
In his late renascence,
Scampering, ancient kitten,
Among soft summer grasses. . .
He held long conversations
With a tail-less friend.
Lovers remember his warm black fur,
Sweet shadow and a ghostly purr.

May Sarton

EMMYCAT

emmy,
one eye
watching the swallows go by,
one eye watching the ghosts

emmycat,
leaping sideways
away from the looming forests
into the wild city streets

Catherin Young

WATCHCAT

Watchcat is wild.
He runs the dark into a hole.
Keep your face away:
He doesn't play.

Watchcat is wild.
He flattens down the sun.
Don't touch his fur:
He doesn't purr.

Watchcat is wild.
He eats up all the stars.
Don't walk on his lawn
Or you'll be gone.

Mimi Drake

THE CAT

The cat by magic comes
Through slits of doors or air
To shadow through the rooms
And stalk what is not there.

And thrust outside by night,
With old and formal shout
In frightful guise she fights
The demons all about.

Then soft in sunny days,
Lulled in the leaves she goes.
No face of fiend dismays
Her vulnerable repose.

Ann Stanford

MRS. VANDEGRIFT

Finally it was noticed that among the flurry
of legs
that filled the halls of the library when the
great bronze doors were opened,
moved a small shape
dodging the shoes with feline fluency.
She was the no color of an old hat,
with tiger memories in her pattern.
In some of the staff, the candor of her presence,
her litter
slung heavy in her belly, set up a stiffness. She
must go.
To her historic cult
she was a ringing call to crusade; they
named her Mrs. Vandegrift after a library endowment.
And with the battle raging around her,
during the telling of Cinderella in the Children's
Room, behind a screen
she gave birth to her rabble litter.
There are rats
under the ivy in the park outside.
But not in the library stacks.
Through the narrow aisles, mostly invisible
but swift as a draft, and lethal, moves a small shape
the color of an old hat.

Dorothy Hughes

ONE'S OWN LION

By intimate markings you shall know
a certain wild identity:
by these four rows
or five of whisker holes,

and how the pits line up
both sides of the king-countenance:
from nostrils nobly down to upper lip.

Make no mistake:
if the cat's yours, it's by
design, including facial follicles.
Commit his pattern to fool's heart. Apply
no wide-of-the-mark ear-clip,
color-daub, collar, brand.
Approach him close as a long-standing pun
between the monarch and his jester man.

Then bend,
as though to kiss
these signal separate tense
antennae, hair by hair.
Joker, you dare
embrace majesty. Here, puss!

Norma Farber

PETER

Strong and slippery, built for the midnight grass-party confronted by four cats,
he sleeps his time away—the detached first claw on the foreleg, which corresponds
to the thumb, retracted to its tip; the small tuft of fronds
or katydid-legs above each eye, still numbering the units in each group;
the shadbones regularly set about the mouth, to droop or rise

in unison like the porcupine's quills—motionless. He lets himself be flattened out by gravity, as it were a piece of seaweed tamed and weakened by
exposure to the sun; compelled when extended, to lie
stationary. Sleep is the result of his delusion that one must do as
well as one can for oneself; sleep—epitome of what is to

him as to the average person, the end of life. Demonstrate on him how
the lady caught the dangerous southern snake, placing a forked stick on either
side of its innocuous neck; one need not try to stir
him up; his prune-shaped head and alligator eyes are not a party to the
joke. Lifted and handled, he may be dangled like an eel or set

up on the forearm like a mouse; his eyes bisected by pupils of a pin's
width, are flickeringly exhibited, then covered up. May be? I should say
might have been; when he has been got the better of in a
dream—as in a fight with nature or with cats—we all know it. Profound sleep is
not with him a fixed illusion. Springing about with froglike ac-

curacy, emitting jerky cries when taken in the hands, he is himself
again; to sit caged by the rungs of a domestic chair would be unprofit-
able—human. What is the good of hypocrisy? It
is permissible to choose one's employment, to abandon the wire nail, the
roly-poly, when it shows signs of being no longer a pleas-

ure, to score the adjacent magazine with a double line of
strokes. He can
talk, but insolently says nothing. What of it? When one
is frank, one's very
presence is a compliment. It is clear that he can see
the virtue of naturalness, that he is one of those who
do not regard
the published fact as a surrender. As for the disposi-
tion

invariably to affront, an animal with claws wants to have to
use
them; that eel-like extension of trunk into tail is not an
accident. To
leap, to lengthen out, divide the air—to purloin, to pursue.
To tell the hen: fly over the fence, go in the wrong
way in your perturba-
tion—this is life; to do less would be nothing but
dishonesty.

Marianne Moore

QUORUM PORUM*

In a dark garden, by a dreadful tree,
The Druid Toms were met. They numbered three,
Tab Tiger, Demon Black, and Ginger Hate.
Their forms were tense, their eyes were full of fate;
Save the involuntary caudal thrill,
The horror was that they should sit so still.
An hour of ritual silence passed: then low
And marrow-freezing, Ginger moaned "OROW",
Two horrid syllables of hellish lore,
Followed by deeper silence than before.

Another hour, the tabby's turn is come;
Rigid, he rapidly howls "MUM MUM MUM";
Then reassumes his silence like a pall,
Clothed in negation, a dumb oracle.
At the third hour, the black gasps out "AH BLURK!"
Like a lost soul that founders in the murk;
And the grim, ghastly, damned and direful crew
Resumes its voiceless vigilance anew.
The fourth hour passes. Suddenly all three
Chant "WEGGY WEGGY WEGGY" mournfully,
Then stiffly rise, and melt into the shade,
Their Sabbath over, and their demons laid.

Ruth Pitter

**Porum*: Genitive plural of "Puss".

CABAL OF CAT AND MOUSE

He has a way, the cat, who sits
on the short grass in lamplight.
Him you could appreciate, and more—
how the musky night fits him,
like a glove; how he adapts down there,
below boughs, to his velvet arena.

His, for playing in. A shadow
plodding past his white paws
could be a swad of anything;
except that, as it bolts, he retrieves
and has tenderly couched it,
and must unroll alongside, loving.

His paws dab and pat at it; his
austere head swivels at an angle
to the barrel neck. Prone, he eyes
its minutest move; his haunch relaxing
parades tolerance, for the pose entreats
doubly to play—it is energy

involved, if you like, in a tacit exchange
of selves, as the cat flares up again,
and has seized what he seizes.
And acts proud, does a dance, for it is
his appetite puts all the mouse into a mouse;
the avid mouse, untameable,

bound by so being to concur,
in his bones, with the procedure.
Even the end cannot cancel that.
The shift from play to kill, measured,
is not advertised. He has applied
a reserved gram of tooth power,

to raise this gibbering curt squeal
at last, and now glassily gazes down.
Plunged, barked as if punched,
and has axed his agitator. You heard
soon the headbones crunch; and you shrank,
the spine exploding like a tower in air.

Christopher Middleton

3.

MYSTERIOUS

CATS

No-one but indefatigable lovers and old
Chilly philosophers can understand the true
Charm of these animals serene and potent, who
Likewise are sedentary and suffer from the cold.

They are the friends of learning and of sexual bliss;
Silence they love, and darkness where temptation breeds.
Erebus would have made them his funereal steeds,
Save that their proud free nature would not stoop to this.

Like those great sphinxes lounging through eternity
In noble attitudes upon the desert sand,
They gaze incuriously at nothing, calm and wise.

Their fecund loins give forth electric flashes, and
Thousands of golden particles drift ceaselessly,
Like galaxies of stars, in their mysterious eyes.

Charles Baudelaire
(translated by George Dillon)

CAT ON THE PORCH AT DUSK

Near the edge, as on a shelf,
The patient cat combines himself.
Motionless he huddles there
Before the changing light, and broods
On daylight's deep ineptitudes.

When gradually the night takes place
He rises, stretching whiskers, toes
And stepping royally, he goes . . .
Slowly the darkness slides apart
And soundless, lets him in.

Dorothy Harriman

CHANG McTANG McQUARTER CAT

Chang McTang McQuarter Cat
Is one part this and one part that.
One part is yowl, one part is purr.
One part is scratch, one part is fur.
One part, maybe even two,
Is how he sits and stares right through
You and you and you and you.
And when you feel my Chang-Cat stare
You wonder if you're really there.

Chang McTang McQuarter Cat
Is one part this and ten parts that.
He's one part saint, and two parts sin.
One part yawn, and three parts grin,
One part sleepy, four parts lightning,
One part cuddly, five parts fright'ning,
One part snarl, and six parts play.
One part is how he goes away
Inside himself, somewhere miles back
Behind his eyes, somewhere as black
And green and yellow as the night
A jungle makes in full moonlight.

Chang McTang McQuarter Cat
Is one part this and twenty that.
One part is statue, one part tricks—
(One part, or six, or thirty-six.)

One part (or twelve, or sixty-three)
Is—Chang McTang belongs to ME!

Don't ask, "How many parts is that?"
Addition's nothing to a cat.

If you knew Chang, then you'd know this:
He's one part everything there is.

John Ciardi

DOUBLE DUTCH

That crafty cat, a buff-black Siamese
Sniffing through wild wood, sagely, silently goes
Prick ears, lank legs, alertly twitching nose,
And on her secret errand reads with ease
A language no man knows.

Walter de la Mare

(MIAO),* 妙

I put down my book
The Meaning of Zen
and see the cat smiling
    into her fur
as she delicately combs it
    with her rough pink tongue.

"Cat, I would lend you this
    book to study
but it appears that you have
    already read it."

She looks up and gives me
    her full gaze.
"Don't be ridiculous," she purrs.
    "I wrote it."

Dilys Laing

**Miao*: Excellent, mysterious, subtle

CATS AND ZINNIAS

The affinity
between cats and zinnias
is a necessary undeclared sufficiency.

Consider
the tall maroon zinnia
unphallicized aristocrat of democracy.
Consider the crossed paws
and the detached indifferent humor
as of aged disillusioned celibate bishops
somnolent in moist lavender afternoons.
(Cats and zinnias cling alike to episcopal palaces,
indifferent alike to tall sunflowers in slum alleys
to orchids over young gin-drenched bellies—
My Lord Bishop, relishing only Scotch,
boredly wiped the unwelcome perfume from the kissed ring—
and cats and zinnias equally
are unconcerned
with tea and holy water.)

Let philosophers talk of
the democracy of rain and starlight
falling equally on American senators in plug hats
and Shriner pins
and Bantu chiefs in plug hats
and gold nose rings.

In the sun-speckled garden
of the episcopal palace
the tall maroon zinnia
and the tall white cat
with green eyes slit like leaves of zinnias seen sidewise
discuss the tall studied indifferent forgotten democracy
of tall indifferent cool Thomas Jefferson thatched like a
    maroon zinnia
equality for the independent purposes
of cats and zinnias.

Zinnias and cats
are equivalent democrats.
Zinnias and cats
are a detached sufficiency,
of cool liberty.

Nelson Antrim Crawford

THE LOST BLACK-AND-WHITE CAT

Cockcrowing at midnight. Broken
silence. Crickets skillfully re-
forming it in
                    minims and
quavers.   The child turns, bangs
      the headboard, struggles
with dreams. Last night in dreams
he found the cat in the bathroom.

                    Come back, cat.
Thrash the silence with your autonomous
feather tail. Imagination made fur,
come back, spring poems out of the whole
cloth of silence.

Denise Levertov

NEW CAT

On neutral territory, a vacant lot next door,
the new cat waits, seemingly indifferent,
among weeds and coke-bottles.
Idly he watches a moth,
      pulls a seedpod from his tail,
            arranges it, a rhythmic oval,
around his body.

The resident cats,
    bellies black and grey close to the ground,
        advance,
            their whiskers crackling tense,
    stop, turned to bronze,
move again,
    meet, nose to nose.
The new cat waits, regally composed.
    Black cat stares long into a gopherhole,
        dips a foreleg to its depth—
the new cat waits.
    Now Grey has reached him,
        nudges lightly,
            turns and moves away.
Black hesitates a moment, then decides to follow.
    The new cat stretches, yawns into the sun,
        curves neatly into a dune-like mound
            and slowly melts into the sand.

Lisl Auf der Heide

THE CAT ON THE MAT DESERVES A PAT

Colette
Kept Love for a pet,
Brushed its fur as soft as silk,
Gave it saucerfuls of milk,
Taught it all the tricks there are—
But didn't trust it very far.

Phyllis McGinley

DRAWING THE CAT

Makes a platform for himself:
forepaws bent under his chest,

slot-eyes shut in a corniced head,
haunches high like a wing chair,
hindlegs parallel, a sled.

As if on water, low afloat
like a wooden duck: a bundle not
apt to be tipped, so symmetrized
on hidden keel of tail he rides
squat, arrested, glazed.

Lying flat, a violin:
hips are splayed, head and chin
sunk on paws, stem straight out
from the arched root
at the clef-curve of the thighs.

Wakes: the head rises.
Claws sprawl. Wires
go taut, make a wicket of his spine.
He humps erect, with scimitar yawn
of hooks and needles porcupine.

Sits, solid as a doorstop,
tail-encircled, tip laid on his toes,
ear-tabs stiff, gooseberry eyes
full, unblinking, sourly wise.
In outline: a demijohn with a pewter look.

Swivels, bends a muscled neck:
petal-of-tulip-tongue slicks
the brushpoint of his tail to black,
then smooths each glossy epaulette
with assiduous sponge.

Whistle him into a canter
into the kitchen: tail hooked aside,
ears at the ready. Elegant copy
of carrousel pony—
eyes bright as money.

May Swenson

THE SECRET IN THE CAT

I took my cat apart
to see what made him purr.
Like an electric clock
or like the snore

of a warming kettle,
something fizzed and sizzled in him.
Was he a soft car,
the engine bubbling sound?

Was there a wire beneath his fur,
or humming throttle?
I undid his throat.
Within was no stir.

I opened up his chest
as though it were a door:
no whisk or rattle there.
I lifted off his skull:

no hiss or murmur.
I halved his little belly
but found no gear,
no cause for static.

So I replaced his lid,
laced his little gut.
His heart into his vest I slid
and buttoned up his throat.

His tail rose to a rod
and beckoned to the air.
Some voltage made him vibrate
warmer than before.

Whiskers and a tail:
perhaps they caught
some radar code
emitted as a pip, a dot-and-dash

of woolen sound.
My cat a kind of tuning fork?—
amplifier?—telegraph?—
doing secret signal work?

His eyes elliptic tubes:
there's a message in his stare.
I stroke him
but cannot find the dial.

May Swenson

COLLOQUY

In the broken light, in owl weather,
Webs on the lawn where the leaves end,
I took the thin moon and the sky for cover
To pick the cat's brains and descend
A weedy hill. I found him grovelling
Inside the summerhouse, a shadowed bulge,
Furred and somnolent. "I bring,"
I said, "beside this dish of liver and an edge
Of cheese, the customary torments,
And the usual wonder why we live
At all, and why the world thins out and perishes
As it has done for me, sieved
As I am toward the silences. Where
Are we now? Do we know anything?"
Now, on another night, his look endures.
"Give me the dish," it said.
I had his answer, wise as yours.

Weldon Kees

IN HONOUR OF TAFFY TOPAZ

Taffy, the topaz-coloured cat,
Thinks now of this and now of that,
But chiefly of his meals.
Asparagus, and cream, and fish
Are objects of his Freudian wish;
What you don't give, he steals

His gallant heart is strongly stirred
By chink of plate or flight of bird,
He has a plumy tail;
At night he treads of stealthy pad
As merry as Sir Galahad
A-seeking of the Grail.

His amiable amber eyes
Are very friendly, very wise;
Like Buddha, grave and fat,
He sits, regardless of applause,
And thinking, as he kneads his paws,
What fun to be a cat!

Christopher Morley

THE MYSTERIOUS CAT

I saw a proud, mysterious cat,
I saw a proud, mysterious cat,
Too proud to catch a mouse or rat—
Mew, mew, mew.

But catnip she would eat, and purr,
But catnip she would eat, and purr.
And goldfish she did much prefer—
Mew, mew, mew.

I saw a cat—'twas but a dream,
I saw a cat—'twas but a dream,
Who scorned the slave that brought her cream—
Mew, mew, mew.

Unless the slave were dressed in style,
Unless the slave were dressed in style,
And knelt before her all the while—
Mew, mew, mew.

Did you ever hear of a thing like that?
Did you ever hear of a thing like that?
Did you ever hear of a thing like that?
Oh, what a proud, mysterious cat,
Oh, what a proud, mysterious cat,
Oh, what a proud, mysterious cat.

Mew . . . Mew . . . Mew.

Vachel Lindsay

THE CAT

Within that porch, across the way,
I see two naked eyes this night;
Two eyes that neither shut nor blink,
Searching my face with a green light.

But cats to me are strange, so strange—
I cannot sleep if one is near;
And though I'm sure I see those eyes,
I'm not so sure a body's there!

W. H. Davies

CAT ON COUCH

My cat, washing her tail's tip, is a whorl
Of white shell,
As perfect as a fan
In full half-moon . . . Next moment she's a hare;
The muzzle softens, rounds, goes dumb, and one
Tall ear dips, falters forward . . . Then,
Cross as switches, she's a great horned owl;
Two leafy tricornered ears reverse, a frown
Darkens her chalky visage, big eyes round
And round and stare down midnight.
                    There sits my cat
Mysterious as gauze,—now somnolent,
No jocose, quicksilver from a dropped
Thermometer. When poised
Below the sketched ballet—
Dancers who pirouette upon the wall,
Calmly she lifts the slim
Boom of her leg, what will
The prima ballerina next
Perform?—Grace held in readiness,
She meditates, a vision of repose.

Barbara Howes

CAT

Again and again through the day
I meet a cat.
In the tree's shade, in the sun, in the crowding brown leaves.
After the success of a few fish bones

Or inside a skeleton of white earth
I find it, as absorbed in the purring
Of its own heart as a bee.
Still it sharpens its claws on the *gulmohar* tree
And follows the sun all day long.

Now I see it and then it is gone,
Losing itself somewhere.
On an autumn evening I have watched it play,
Stroking the soft body of the saffron sun
With a white paw. Then it caught
The darkness in paws like small balls
And scattered it all over the earth.

Jibanananda Das
(*translated by* Lila Ray)

FOR A YELLOW CAT AT MIDNIGHT

As though drifted inland
in some dark current of your own,
you settle against my side,
cumbrous as clay or a warm stone,
and I wake to find you there.

Why at night, small lion,
are you so much heavier than by day?
Only this afternoon
you slept, upside down, in a lap
already full of books and child,
and you were a tawny feather,
a fluff of sun.

Now pulled hard to the earth's center,
as though to a final place,
(lion, are we older by a night?)
we wait for sleep,

held fast by separate stars,
ponderous with what we do not know,
caught in a common dark.

Jean Burden

DEATH OF A CAT

A sultry, summer evening, the children playing jacks
in the hot and grimy garage
under the yellow eyes of their grey cat,
when the rubbery jack ball
popped like a bubble into the street
And the cocky cat after its red-streaking path.

Brakes scrunched, the cat shot up like a spark,
hit harshly over a tilted ear,
and the cross-legged children screamed
at the driven death of their pet.
While I hauled a hose to clean
The clotted pavement stains, I thought of an ancient legend.

In the Irish Golden Age, three fasting clerks on pilgrimage
sailed hungrily off to sea,
praying with soft and folded hands
their serene faith in God's care.
But the young clerk said in his caution,
"I think I will take the silence of my small grey cat."

On the rocky shore of an island, they beached the boat
and kneeled to speak the Psalms;
the cat crept to a wild wave
and snatched a salmon from the foam.
Still the clerks doubted the Lord's hand
Until the fish began to burn upon a sudden fire of coals.

Kneeling shadowy on the oily pavement, I saw
some jelly of the cat's lost brain,
a little mound of curious cells
clinging against the asphalt veins
and fountainhead of lashing water.
On the hose's full fury washed the cells away.

The myth of the showering, supernal claw grew old
in the grey silence of evening,
lost in the glittering air;
though as water smashed the cells,
they flickered in tingling twilight
Like sparks snapping through the foam of a fire.

James Schevill

THE RABBIT AS KING OF THE GHOSTS

The difficulty to think at the end of day,
When the shapeless shadow covers the sun
And nothing is left except light on your fur—

There was the cat slopping its milk all day,
Fat cat, red tongue, green mind, white milk
And August the most peaceful month.

To be, in the grass, in the peacefullest time,
Without that monument of cat,
The cat forgotten in the moon;

And to feel that the light is a rabbit-light,
In which everything is meant for you
And nothing need be explained;

Then there is nothing to think of. It comes of itself;
And east rushes west and west rushes down,
No matter. The grass is full

And full of yourself. The trees around are for you,
The whole of the wideness of night is for you,
A self that touches all edges,

You become a self that fills the four corners of night.
The red cat hides away in the fur-light
And there you are humped high, humped up,

You are humped higher and higher, black as stone—
You sit with your head like a carving in space
And the little green cat is a bug in the grass.

Wallace Stevens

WAITING FOR *IT*

My cat jumps to the window sill
and sits there still as a jug.
He's waiting for me, but I cannot be
coming, for I am in the room.

His snout, a gloomy V of patience,
pokes out into the sun.
The funnels of his ears expect
to be poured full of my footsteps.

It, the electric moment, a sweet
mouse, will appear; at his gray
eye's edge I'll be coming home
if he sits on the window ledge.

It is here, I say, and call him
to my lap. Not a hair
in the gap of his ear moves.
His clay gaze stays steady.

That solemn snout says: *It*
is what is about to happen, not
what is already here.

May Swenson

THE CAT IN THE WINDOW

The cat knows. His whitest shape
In the wide window disturbs my blood,

Disturbs the green that filled my eye
All summer long. His eye is deep

And steady, unburdened by love
Or the thought of glittering wings

High in the glare of northern ice.
I would like to watch the cat,

To understand such easiness,
But the day is filled with a late flaming air.

North of me, the storms are ganging up.
There is a yellow rattling in the wind.

I walk away, return, leave again,
But all day long I imagine the cat

As falling leaves, falling snow;
As something that flows over me

With quiet, almost careless grace.

Harry Humes

CAT AT NIGHT

Across from him the cat
Lies sleeping in the captain's chair.
It moves slightly; ripples stir
Its gray and white shape
Like wind on deepest ponds.
The room seems to begin
In such repose,
In such a quiet swirling.

Outside he hears September ending;
A moth bangs against the window screen;
Raccoons scream across the fields.

He looks at the cat, at the head,
The ears, the shoulders, legs,
The pads and hidden claws . . .
It's like seeing further
Than the eye allows.

But then the cat rises, stretches,
Stands arched over the night.
For a moment it sees him
With eyes dark with almost meaning . . .

. . . it settles like mist,
Curls toward sleep again,
Like something he almost missed.

Harry Humes

TIPSIE

Oriental Princess
                    We call her
Oriental Princess of the Quarter Moon
      White kitten
                    Not as long as her name
White with a black quarter moon on her brow
      Moon for short
Or Tipsie for the black tip of her tail
      We try to be one with her
But she is a very private person
      Her treasure a kitten-sized skip rope
                    She secures between
                         Her somewhat teeth
Hides it from us
      Whenever she stops skipping
In the shower stall back of the stereo
                    Behind the radiator
Now we don't know where
      We can afford our princess privacy
                    Princess of the Quarter Moon

Emilie Glen

ANIMALS WANT TO KNOW

Animals want to know
what we think

they are.

They wonder
what we are

going to say.

A cat does
not want
flattery
lying

on the stair

licking
a dead lizard.

Spitting
the feathers
of a blackbird

found
in the yard.

He doesn't
desire praise
from us
unless we mean it

and we sit
looking at the cat
for days

quiet days
that pass
without a word.

George Keithley

A TROUBLED SLEEP

My cats in their huddled sleep
(Two heaps of fur made one)
Twitch their ears and whimper—
Do they dream the same dream?

Something's upset them both!
What's leering through the dark
Wherein they're so entwined
They shudder through each other,

Two creatures so involved
(Cat sister and cat brother)
They can but share as one
What nightmare shakes the other?

And yet I've watched them creep,
Each one intent, alone,
Drawn to a single focus,
So passionately its own

Objective that they'd spit
(Cat sister or cat brother)
On which one dared presume
To trespass near the other.

I think the latter scene
(The unit not the plus)
Becomes both him and her
More than this unquiet fur

Of cats anonymous—
Even though they stalk a bird
That holds my breath to pray
It safely flies away—
I like them better thus.

Eric Barker

FOR ONE WHO LIVES WITH ME

I'll move like a lion,
like water, like music,
I'll crouch like the Sphinx,
sit like Buddha,

sleep in a compact
circle of gold,
still as the sun,
as radiant.

And you, my sister,
my teacher in fur,
will stare your approval
and call me brother.

Francis Maguire

SLEEPING CATS

My fat, black cat,
Who was once a man,
Was wild and scarey.
He was Ghengis Khan.
He ranted and he raved;
It was never tedious.
You can learn all about him
In Encyclopedias.

My grey, striped cat,—
She was Cleopatra.
She floated on a barge
From Siam to Sumatra,

A barge. all gold,
And cushions, and pearls,
With twenty-seven Oarsmen
And no other girls.

Now my two old creatures
Sleep where the sun is streaming
And I wonder and wonder
And wonder what they're dreaming.

Jean Pedrick

CINNAMON THE CAT

His a more mysterious spice
than common condiment,
his giving is not sharp
or quickened with the easy, trite
flow of salt and pepper's black and white,
for he is golden.

He faces you a bit apart,
contemplative.
He meditates.
His eyes are more than sad
as if beneath all feeling
were all knowing.

To end an interview
he turns his back and sits
motionless
a Buddha
except his ears that twitch to catch
what comes or goes behind him.

For those of quiet taste
he has a subtle flavor
unforgettable.

Hortense Roberta Roberts

SYMPOSIUM

The cat is a complicated beast;
he trails his thoughts in various directions,
considering which and what and why
before he makes a move.

I do not agree with you—
the cat's mind snaps and acts.
Without meditation he pounces—
considering afterward that he's done well.

Ah, you both are wrong!
The cat is far too wise to either act in haste
or linger overlong. He does as wise men do—
breaks his bread, gives thought to thought,
and slumbers in his song.

Ruth Munch

A CERTAIN WISDOM

You curl the silence of your sleep,
one velvet paw curved like a shell
scooping an intrinsic substance
to cover your eyes.

I watch you in your world
and I grow wise.

You are a golden flash
that singles itself in shadows.
You carve your domain
from fence to house
then gather the rooms about you

for your own.
Each of your days is a world.

You do not look back on yesterday
nor do you anticipate tomorrow.
You live the present intensified
in its own way,
and trust my every circling of your world.

Ruth Munch

CAT

downstairs one floor
colored like old brass
glides like water over the grass
to rub my leg.
Maine small town summer landscape
changes to dusk.
The cat steals off to try out,
just for size,
the cardboard boxes I've stored in the barn.
Comes back.
We sit like jugs
and watch an old man,
in dungarees and green work shirt,
steer up the street on the end of his pipe.
Nobody near, I say to the cat
in a voice louder than a whisper:
"I won't tell anybody that you can talk,"
and look to the bottoms of his green eyes
that do not tell
what he feels, sees, hears, sighs.

George Barr

DIALOGUE

Cat,
Why do you look at me like that?
What have I done that I evoke
Such clear, such agate-cold contempt?
Am I that poor a joke?

In your cat-sight I suppose I am.
Look what I do:
Invent the legend that I think,
And think things through
To ends I tell myself are fine,
Important, logical, immense;
Wear myself out walking the line
(Narrower than the slits are in your eyes)
Between spirit and sense,
Self and self-sacrifice,
Free-will and doom
And in the little room left over,
Work for my play, and play being lover.
(Oh all right—*scratch*! That cushion needs a cover.)

Now let's take you:
You are the sphinx—
Or so at least my whole race thinks
Who sees you come and go at will,
Play with a thread,
Sit dead still by the hour in grass
Which may, with luck, produce one mouse.
For this: free bed,
free board, freedom to insult me in my house.
What do you think, my sphinx, of that?
It is for this that Egypt had a cult
Of cat?

You see there's somewhere a great fallacy:
You think you're free; I know I'm not.
I love you for this fine pretense,

This act as if you didn't care a whit
If doors are shut, your food too cold, too hot—
You are a master of expedience
But—wise?
No—in spite of evidential eyes:
In love you cry like us and moan
But, I aver,
In giving birth we know enough to groan;
You purr.

Evelyn Ames

THE CAT

He has a history
of long, silent
descending
from trees.
He lands

years later
in the laps of women.
He brings with him
a memory
of waiting deep in leaves,

of bright claws he now
is amazed to find
grown short and tucked
like pale fingers
into the folds of a dress.

He has fallen
out of life.

He tries to remember
a lake in a clearing,
but each time he would drink

from that memory
he discovers
in a blue saucer of milk
his face like a head
served up on a plate.

Philip Dacey

RADAR SCREEN

The scoop of the cat's ear
catches sounds small enough
to go through a sieve, a screen
a fine mesh. The scoop
swerves toward a noise capturing it
with a flick either to keep it
in a little bin of knowledge or
to toss it out with another flick
ready to scoop again any time.

Jean Harper

CONCORD CATS

The soft cat and the scratchy cat
Have milk in cold blue plates.
Then, in evenings, star-cool evenings
Equal to their reticence,
Emblems of independence.

These China cats, of black and white,
Will go on planetary pads
Uphill, where crouch
On eighteenth-, seventeenth-century
Houses, the graves of Concord.

My pious inscriptions
That antedate the Revolution
They see, through eyes cold and chaste,
The scratchy cat, the soft cat,
With humor old and Oriental,

That nature is meant for poise.
Battles, bloodshed, death,
Are men mirroring time,—
The stars blue, the night paling—
Are data. Imperviousness. Integrity.

Richard Eberhart

VILLANELLE FOR THE CAT

My supple ways are deep as water's ways.
The moves I make embody what I know.
I lift my paw and trace a secret sign.

I have a history of blood and grace.
I honor it by pacing to and fro.
My subtle ways are deep as water's ways.

I move in keeping with a god's design.
I'm moving quickest when I'm moving slow.
I lift my paw and make a secret sign.

My body translates mysteries with ease.
My body is the Book of How to Go.
I swear my ways are deep as water's ways.

I send a message with my arching spine
But keep back more a message than I show.
I lift my paw and give a secret sign.

By feinting at a ghost I offer praise.
I recognize what's high by crouching low.
My supple ways are deep as water's ways.
I lift my paw and trace a secret sign.

Philip Dacey

4.

ANTIC

THE NAMING OF CATS

The Naming of Cats is a difficult matter,
    It isn't just one of your holiday games;
You may think at first I'm as mad as a hatter
When I tell you, a cat must have THREE DIFFERENT NAMES.
First of all, there's the name that the family use daily,
    Such as Peter, Augustus, Alonzo or James,
Such as Victor or Jonathan, George or Bill Bailey—
    All of them sensible everyday names.
There are fancier names if you think they sound sweeter,
    Some for the gentlemen, some for the dames:
Such as Plato, Admetus, Electra, Demeter—
    But all of them sensible everyday names.
But I tell you, a cat needs a name that's particular.
    A name that's peculiar, and more dignified,
Else how can he keep up his tail perpendicular,
    Or spread out his whiskers, or cherish his pride?
Of names of this kind I can give you a quorum,
    Such as Munkustrap, Quaxo, or Coricopat,
Such as Bombalurina, or else Jellylorum—
    Names that never belong to more than one cat.
But above and beyond there's still one name left over,
    And that is the name that you never will guess;
The name that no human research can discover—
    But the CAT HIMSELF KNOWS, and will never confess.
When you notice a cat in profound meditation,
    The reason, I tell you, is always the same:
His mind is engaged in a rapt contemplation
    Of the thought, of the thought of the thought of his name:
        His ineffable effable
        Effanineffable
Deep and inscrutable singular Name.

T. S. Eliot

MY CAT, MRS. LICK-A-CHIN

Some of the cats I know about
Spend a little time in and a lot of time out.
Or a lot of time out and a little time in.
By *my* cat, Mrs. Lick-a-chin,
Never knows *where* she wants to be.
If I let her in she looks at me
And begins to sing that she wants to go out.
So I open the door and she looks about
And begins to sing, "Please let me in!"

Poor silly Mrs. Lick-a-chin!

The thing about cats as you may find,
Is that no one knows what they have in mind.

And I'll tell you something about that:
No one knows it less than my cat.

John Ciardi

THE OWL AND THE PUSSY-CAT

The Owl and the Pussy-Cat went to sea
    In a beautiful pea-green boat,
They took some honey and plenty of money
    Wrapped up in a five-pound note.
The Owl looked up to the stars above,
    And sang to a small guitar,
"O lovely Pussy! O Pussy, my love,
    What a beautiful Pussy you are,
        You are,
        You are!
What a beautiful Pussy you are!"

Pussy said to the Owl, "You elegant fowl!
    How charmingly sweet you sing!
O let us be married! Too long we have tarried:
    But what shall we do for a ring?"
They sailed away for a year and a day,
    To the land where the Bong-tree grows,
And there in a wood a Piggy-wig stood,
    With a ring at the end of his nose,
        His nose,
        His nose,
    With a ring at the end of his nose.

"Dear Pig, are you willing to sell for one shilling
    Your ring?" Said the Piggy, "I will."
So they took it away, and were married next day
    By the Turkey who lives on the hill.
They dined on mince, and slices of quince,
    Which they ate with a runcible spoon;
And hand in hand, on the edge of the sand,
    They danced by the light of the moon,
        The moon,
        The moon,
    They danced by the light of the moon.

Edward Lear

A CAT MAY LOOK AT A KING

The cat
    Came and sat
    Down before His Majesty;
The Cat
Came and sat
    Down before the King.

"I've come to take a look,
For unless I am mistook,
It is written in a book,
    I may do this thing!"

She took
Quite a look
    Over all His Majesty;
She took
Quite a look,
    And then she shook her head.
"There's little here to praise,
Plain his looks and dull his ways;
I'll turn my loving gaze
    On Tabby Tom instead!"

Laura E. Richards

CAT

Cats are not at all like people
        Cats are Cats.

People wear stockings and sweaters,
Overcoats, mufflers, and hats.
Cats wear nothing: they lie by the fire
For twenty-four hours if they desire.
They do NOT rush out to the office,
They do NOT have interminable chats,
They do NOT play Old Maid and Checkers,
They do NOT wear bright yellow spats.

People of course, will always be people,
        But Cats are Cats.

William Jay Smith

A LITERARY CAT

(Not you,
My draggletail disaster),
Hodge was a cat
worth looking at.
Dr. Sam Johnson
was his master.
Boswell
Immortalized him, too.
(Not you, Sourpuss.
Hardly you.)

Helen Bevington

LITTLE GIRL CAT

Little girl cat, made for me,
Her long ears listening to street noises,
Her sharp teeth smiling.

My cat, molded on a stand,
A carved spider,
Alert at my fireplace.

I held her paw three times,
And she began to dance,
Began to dress, my cat,

A firefly in spurts of whiskers;
Danced in the outside air,
Bruised her ear, my cat,

Was sent to a wood hospital
On a pillow . . . poor pussy willow,
Pranced away, my practiced cat.

My cat has a wire tail and wooden ears,
A sylph-like animal with a zig-zag spring,
Standing on woman's legs.

My cat has wings for fuzz,
She purrs at my artificial fireplace,
My wild bird, my lady cat.

Hy Sobiloff

THE CAT

You get a wife, you get a house,
Eventually you get a mouse.
You get some words regarding mice,
You get a kitty in a trice.
By two A.M. or thereabout,
The mouse is in, the cat is out.
It dawns upon you, in your cot,
The mouse is silent, the cat is not.
Instead of Pussy, says your spouse,
You should have bought another mouse.

Ogden Nash

THE TOO FAT CAT

A cat came by
And asked of me
If I would brew her
Some catnip tea.

"I'm sorry," I said,
"I've none in the house,
But how would you like
A scalloped mouse?

"Or wouldn't you love
A sparrow on toast,
Or a bowl of cream,
Or goldfish roast?"

"I'm dieting now,"
Sadly mewed she,
"And I must have nothing
But catnip tea."

Elaine V. Emans

VERSES ON A CAT

I

A cat in distress,
Nothing more, nor less;
Good folks, I must faithfully tell ye,
As I am a sinner,
It waits for some dinner
To stuff out its own little belly.

II

You would not easily guess
All the modes of distress
Which torture the tenants on earth;
And the various evils,
Which like so many devils,
Attend the poor souls from their birth.

III

Some a living require,
And others desire
An old fellow out of the way;
And which is the best
I leave to be guessed,
For I cannot pretend to say.

IV

One wants society,
Another variety,
Others a tranquil life;
Some want food,
Others, as good,
Only want a wife.

V

But this poor little cat
Only wanted a rat,
To stuff out its own little maw;
And it was as good
Some people had such food,
To make them *hold their jaw*!

Percy Bysshe Shelley

UNDER-THE-TABLE-MANNERS

It's very hard to be polite
If you're a cat.
When other folks are up at table
Eating all that they are able,
You are down upon the mat
If you're a cat.

You're expected just to sit
    If you're a cat.
Not to let them know you're there
By scratching at the chair,
    Or a light, respected pat
    If you're a cat.

You are not to make a fuss
    If you're a cat.
Tho' there's fish upon the plate
You're expected just to wait,
    Wait politely on the mat
    If you're a cat.

Anon.

DIAMOND CUT DIAMOND

Two cats
One up a tree
One under the tree
The cat up a tree is he
The cat under the tree is she
The tree is witch elm, just incidentally.
He takes no notice of she, she takes no notice of he.
He stares at the woolly clouds passing, she stares at the tree.
There's been a lot written about cats, by old Possum, Yeats and Company
But not Alfred de Musset or Lord Tennyson or Poe or anybody
Wrote about one cat under, and one cat up, a tree.
God knows why this should be left for me
Except I like cats as cats be
Especially one cat up
And one cat under
A witch elm
Tree

Ewart Milne

THE AD-DRESSING OF CATS

You've read of several kinds of Cat,
And my opinion now is that
You should need no interpreter
To understand their character.
You now have learned enough to see
That Cats are much like you and me
And other people whom we find
Possessed of various kinds of mind.
For some are sane and some are mad
And some are good and some are bad
And some are better, some are worse—
But all may be described in verse.
You've seen them both at work and games,
And learnt about their proper names,
Their habits and their habitat:
But

How would you ad-dress a Cat?

So first, your memory I'll jog,
And say: A CAT IS NOT A DOG.

Now Dogs pretend they like to fight;
They often bark, more seldom bite;
But yet a Dog is, on the whole,
What you would call a simple soul.
Of course I'm not including Pekes,
And such fantastic canine freaks.
The usual Dog about the Town
Is much inclined to play the clown,
And far from showing too much pride
Is frequently undignified.
He's very easily taken in—
Just chuck him underneath the chin
Or slap his back or shake his paw,
And he will gambol and guffaw.
He's such an easy-going lout,

He'll answer any hail or shout.
Again I must remind you that
A Dog's a Dog—a CAT'S A CAT.

With Cats, some say, one rule is true:
Don't speak till you are spoken to.
Myself, I do not hold with that—
I say, you should ad-dress a Cat.
But always keep in mind that he
Resents familiarity.
I bow, and taking off my hat,
Ad-dress him in this form: O CAT!
But if he is the cat next door,
Whom I have often met before
(He comes to see me in my flat)
I greet him with an OOPSA CAT!
I think I've heard them call him James—
But we've not got so far as names.
Before a Cat will condescend
To treat you as a trusted friend,
Some little token of esteem
Is needed, like a dish of cream;
And you might now and then supply
Some caviare, or Strassburg Pie,
Some potted grouse, or salmon paste—
He's sure to have his personal taste.
(I know a Cat who makes a habit
Of eating nothing else but rabbit,
And when he's finished, licks his paws
So's not to waste the onion sauce.)
A Cat's entitled to expect
These evidences of respect.
And so in time you reach your aim,
And finally call him by his NAME.

So this is this, and that is that:
And here's how you AD-DRESS A CAT.

T. S. Eliot

THE KILKENNY CATS

There wanst was two cats at Kilkenny,
Each thought there was one cat too many,
  So they quarrell'd and fit,
  They scratched and they bit,
  Till, excepting their nails,
  And the tips of their tails,
Instead of two cats, there warnt any.

Anon.

Mehitabel finds a home

well now it
looks as if
mehitabel the cat
might be on the
way toward a
reform or if not
a reform at least
on the way toward
domestication of some
sort some young
artists who live in
their studio
in the greenwich
village section
of new york city
have taken pity
on her destitution
and have adopted
her this is the
life archy she says
i am living on

condensed milk and
synthetic gin hoopla
for the vie de boheme
exclamation point

there s nothing bourgeois
about those people
that have taken
me in archy i
have been there
a week and have
not yet seen them
go to bed
except in the daytime
a party every night
and neither
the piano lid
nor the ice-box lid
ever closed
kitty said my new
mistress to me
yesterday you are
welcome here so long
as you don t
raise a family
but the first
kitten that i hear
mewing on these
premises back to
the alley for you
it is a comfort to
know there are some
live ones left in
these melancholy days
and while the
humans are dancing
in the studio
i get some of my

feline friends
and we sing
and dance on the
skylight to gehenna
with the bourgeois
bunch that locks
their ice boxes
archy when i lead my
gang into the
apartment at
four in the morning
there are no bolts
or bars anywhere
and not an
inhibition on the place
i feel little
archy that i have
come home to my own
kith and kin
again after
years of fruitless
wandering archy

Don Marquis

CAT & THE WEATHER

Cat takes a look at the weather:
snow;
puts a paw on the sill;
his perch is piled, is a pillow.

Shape of his pad appears:
will it dig? No,
not like sand,
like his fur almost.

But licked, not liked:
too cold.
Insects are flying, fainting down.
He'll try

to bat one against the pane.
They have no body and no buzz,
and now his feet are wet;
it's a puzzle.

Shakes each leg,
then shakes his skin
to get the white flies off;
looks for his tail,

tells it to come on in
by the radiator.
World's turned queer
somehow: all white,

no smell. Well, here
inside it's still familiar.
He'll go to sleep until
it puts itself right.

May Swenson

CONCEIT WITH AUNTIES, URN AND PUSS

Beneath the thorn tree's spikey shade
        My aunts sip milk and marmalade,
Throughout the Gothick afternoon
        They dance beneath a sun-shamed moon.

Their cat, a beastly yellow thing,
        Is humming snatches from "The Ring"—
While milky ladies spin and turn
        Before a classic Grecian urn.
And no one thinks my aunts abnormal
        In that English garden formal.
For, gathering by the tulip tree
        They crane, so they may better see
The fluttering veil, the bombazine,
        The peau de soie, the crepe de Chine—
All moving languid as they turn
        Before the cat and formal urn.
Miaow, miaow, miaow, miaow—
        The thing is singing Verdi now.

Michael T. Leech

MY CAT WITH HIS BUTTERFLY EYES

I.

With his eyes of fur in amber
My cat with his barberpole tail
My cat with his flag flying
My cat with his mast quivering like a machine
My cat with his paws of evaporated milk
With his hummingbird paws with his paws of grasshopper
My cat with his telephone toes
With his ears like subways
My cat with his crowded ears
My cat whose ears point toward anger
My cat with his rosebush mouth
My cat with his mouth full of darning needles

With his cigarette teeth
My cat with his mouth of the Chinese language
My cat with his voice like birdseed
My cat with three serious lines
My cat who is a pianist my cat who understands Beethoven
My cat like a motorcycle
My cat like an armful of trains
My cat between mattresses
My cat with his back of a brontosaur
With his back that is like calligraphy
With his artichoke belly
My cat's belly of dandelions and sacks of grain
With his belly like the sun and the moon like everything
That's helpless.

II.

My cat is to lick
My cat is to lick my cat
My cat's eyes are to wake up
My cat's eyes don't believe
They will not be reached behind suitcases
My cat's ears are to put castor oil in
My cat's tail is to catch
My cat's paws are to rollerskate
His claws are to arrange to disarrange
My cat is to hold down to hold up to let go
My cat is to fill up
My cat is to parachute
My cat is to go to the bottom of the garden
To go to the head of the stairs
Bamboo
My cat is to handle like fever like schizophrenia
My cat is to hate me
My cat is to love

Donald Finkel and Constance Urdang

REQUIESCAT

The cat that all night long was a soprano
Despite his sex, which we shall not discuss,
Toward morning, after the long night's inferno
(And it was long), is still melodious.

As all great artists know, whether they favor
The Metropolitan or the back yard,
The cat who lives for song must learn to savor
The horrid truth: the artist's life is hard.

The love-duet in *Tristan und Isolde*
Was unappreciated once, they say—
The love-song we are hearing, though far older,
Is unappreciated still to-day.

The random objects angry hands are flinging
From a dark window, opened quietly,
Halt, at its very height, that tender singing—
This is an act of grave discourtesy.

Four cans, two bottles, are but scant requital
For lofty song, and a distinguished cat,
Whose art is so significant and vital,
Has reason to expect much more than that.

And yet, at dawn, turning the matter over,
We are inclined to feel that, all in all,
A song purely personal to the lover
Is seldom more than merely personal.

John Hall Wheelock

THE LITTLE CATS

Our mackerel cat
Has three kittens.
The girl one sat
With white mittens
Down in the hall.
The grandfather clock
Bonged. The kitten
Shied at the shock.

Pounce, bounce,
Come her two brothers.
There were once
Three others.
We don't surmise
Who their sire is.
Their round eyes
Are all iris.

They sleep in a ball.
They scuffle and scamper.
Once they lived all
By the clothes-hamper.
Of their mother they know
They can't boss her.
They sit in a row
For the milk saucer.

They think a brown marble
Is a mouse.
They hop up stairs
And lurk through the house.

Pretentious books
By many are written.
I prefer the looks
Of a high-tail kitten.

William Rose Benet

TIGGER

Tigger rubs his whiskers against my whiskers
to thank me for the dust he rolls in
and kneads my knees with tree-sharpened claws
to tell me he is the boss.
He spots buttercup butterflies in the autumn leaves
and pretends to keep secrets
from the last of the summer-time bees.
He thinks he hides in the cedar bushes
then flops over in the greenest grass he can find
and makes the afternoon a poem.

H. McAden Burwell

CANTALOUPE CAT

I'm Taurus (bearded bull) he said
an earth sign
   and she is Aries (blonde trailing hair)
a symbol of air
but our ruling house is Venus
and Xuxek (our calico cat)
means Venus in Mayan.

Xuxek sprang from all their high places
teased every tassel, hung on the curtains
nibbled flowers in vases
dumped and sorted the waste paper
and finally consumed the rind of my cantaloupe.
I found her no goddess yet she took
their love in leaps of delight.

Bernice Ames

TWO CATS

It's a cold night. Two cats
kick up their heels in Smith Court
frisky perky coats shining
whiskers at the walrus. Twelve
above zero. No frozen feet here—
not on the ground long enough.
Ice on the sidewalk
sends their rabbit-legs askew,
their comedy act unnoticed
by the passing man huddled
against the cutting wind. The cats
see him though. Quick as thought
they are through the broken cellar door,
their decorative rosebuds
the last things seen of them.
Nothing else now on the short street
but ruts and rubbish—

Jean Harper

CAT CHASING THE FLY

Without a move, he's four feet in the air.
Nijinsky's elevation! Hunter's claws
Go wild to catch the housefly puppeteer
That pulls him into loops, pirouettes
And sets of *grand jetes* across the floor.

Excited open, yellow eyes ring
The tensile pupil holes, like sun explosions
Dancing on the moon's eclipsing rim.

In one long frenzied leap he's on the screen
And has the spirit fly. Stuck, he clutches
There, his eyes gone thin again, and waits
To be unhooked from his triumphant pose.

T. J. Worthington

THE CAT BALLET

Waiting centuries for his mistress
the German Shepherd hunches on the lawn,
blinking in meditation
beside dishes of food and water.
Not alone. The new kitten
more red than white
waits too, in her fashion.

That breathing rock, I'll climb it.
Digging her needles into skin.
Tumbles down with a feline laugh.
Runs to the fenced flowers.
With a jump like wings
returns in a challenging scratch.

Kitten in air after a dandelion puff
hears the growl for a stranger
(dog or man) at the gate.
Streaks to the barking rock . . .
curls up in his paws
like a mandarin orange.

Eve Triem

THE TORTOISE-SHELL SPY

Her pink paw is for poses—
Raise, bend, and beg.
The left, dark business paw
Detains and questions whole coffee beans,
Beats lettuce silly.

"Why?" "Why?" eyes
Plead with her mews.
Silhouette ears sprout
From behind her dark head.
Parabola hips crouch
Like furry black fenders.

Floors, rugs, laps form jumping-off points.
Contract and leap,
She's on the radiator;
Up to the desk, the window,
Then sits, patient as a geranium.

Dennis Donahue

CALICO JUNE

Sitting cross-legged before June
with the country Curé of Bernanos,
I tremble ever so slightly
reading, "It is hard to be alone,"
and a calico paw lands on my page:
my possessive, demanding Cat.

Book forgotten, I allow her
to lead me deeper into June.

A butterfly dips
perilously near the coral nose,
the paw swats, never intending to snare,
and a robin acclaims this flirt
of motion with *cheery-oat*
flutesong.

How the soft green eyes rivet
on the sudden stranger zigzagging
up my bare leg,
in Amish bonnet and on dainty stilts,
such an old world bug,
black as my hair and hurrying:
ah, safe! The whiskers of my fur friend
only tease, and this visitor
streaks for foliage where ants are busy
opening peony gates.
Less safe
that fellow with the trombone legs!
—my pet grows sleek
on grasshopper sweetmeats:
afternoon crackles like popcorn.

Together we regard a spider
shuttling thread in the already
lacy fern,
contemplate a silver ripple
of squirrel
on risky poplar,
eye the nighthawk day-riding,
shifting gears,
zooming
into our calico June.

Now,
She is studying my face.
What can she unearth
beyond the comfortable mask?

The parade of pain's inside
catacombs of brain,
and I'll not let her tangle
in the daisychain of happenings,
where dream is mixed up
with real, weather is weighty,
and the Slough of Despond
is a strange little flicker
of candle bidding the traveler in.

"I'm heavy company for myself
sometime," I quote old Steerforth
to her, carelessly;
but this cat of summer
has caught me red-handed,
her face obscuring
yet defining all my inner climate.
I stroke her gently,
looking down the long hall
of mirrors
in those eyes.

Raymond Roseliep

5.

WILD

THE PANTHER

Jardin des Plantes, Paris

His sight from ever gazing through the bars,
has grown so blunt that it sees nothing more.
It seems to him that thousands of bars are
before him, and behind him nothing merely.

The easy motion of his supple stride,
which turns about the very smallest circle,
is like a dance of strength about a center,
in which a mighty will stands stupefied.

Only sometimes when the pupils film
soundlessly open . . . then one image fills
and glides through the quiet tension of the limbs
into the heart and ceases and is still.

Rainer Maria Rilke
(*translated by* C. F. MacIntyre)

THE PERFECT LION

The perfect lion in the lion's picture
isn't the beast that bellowed in the zoo—
too much is missing—he's become a fixture
of soundless fur, stuffed, for all we know—
the sores he got from rubbing on the bars
are turned, and do not show.

We can't see, either, that his claws are broken—
the pace of pride on concrete wore them low;
not the whole lion, he's the lion's token,
a lying picture such as children view,
who when they hear his jungle thunder spoken,
feel that it is true.

But we are wiser to his yellow eyes—
grey in the picture—that appear so fierce
and quick to catch a shy prey by surprise—
they mirror nothing now but children's fears
and our own pity at his golden gaze
looking out at ours,

the very picture of a useless rage
locked in or out depending on who's who,
and if we see him gnawing in the cage
on rawness such as perfect lions chew
we can be sure that his vestigial ways
are shadows of a glow.

Harold Witt

CATS

Between fangs stronger and more cruel than rock
A striped cat cracks the shoulder of a steer;
Beside a Bengal pool another of the stock
Crunches on the haunches of a deer.

Striped muscles of what strength
On high-pitched feline nerves are strung!
A female of Siberia licks her paw, lying full length,
With circular motion of the tongue.

Beautiful Brazilian with a shower of spots,
Jaguar. Her easy motion of the hips
Is like a woman walking. Limpid her thoughts.
Luxurious as her floral-spots Brazil to which her thought slips.

Black all black, created He them, male and female:
Murderer, the black leopard, spots concealed.
Fixed eyes of hallucination stare till human eyes fail
Till human blood is congealed.

Quietly, quietly, a mountain of sand in a cage.
The lion's sides are as sand, so fine in grain. His name
Is furrowed like furrowed sand. His rage
Is the rage of water beneath sandhills through blasts of rain.

Pearl Andelson Sherry

HOW TO TELL A TIGER

People who know tigers
    Very very well
All agree that tigers
    Are not hard to tell.

The way to tell a tiger is
    With lots of room to spare.
Don't try telling them up close
    Or we may not find you there.

John Ciardi

THE BLACK PANTHER

(from Leconte de Lisle)

Pallors of rose widen across the sky
along its eastern margin crinkles with fresh light,
and, in a shower of drops resolved, merge in the sea
    pearls from the necklace of the night.

Now all one quarter of the sky, sheathed in soft flames,
gathers to gold on the blue glitter of its spire.
One lingering fold, ablush against the green of gems,
    whelms all in dripping rain of fire.

And from the bamboos that wake against the beating wings
of wind, and lichees purple-fruited, and upon
cinnamon trees where dews are bunched in glittering
    globes, swarm the fresh murmurs of the dawn.

From wood and hillside, flowers, from height of moss
    along
the soft and subtle atmosphere, begins a flight,
from air suddenly troubled, of odors sweet and strong,
    fevered with promise of delight.

There, where all paths are lost in virgin growth of trees
and thick grass steams against the sun in morning glades,
by streams quick-running deep between declivities,
    beneath rattans in green arcades,

she goes, the queen of Java, the dark huntress. Dawn
sees her return to the lair, where her little ones
disconsolately yowl heap-huddled, one upon
    another, nested in shining bones.

Watchful, with eyes barbed like arrows, in sinuous stride
she walks among the glooms of heavy boughs, restless,
with fresh blood spattered here and there along her side
    and damp upon her velvet dress.

She drags with her a remnant of the beast she killed
and fed on in the night, quarter and half the back
of a grand stag. On moss and flower, grim traces spilled,
    red, wet, and warm still, stain her track.

Above, brown bees and butterflies, in rivalry
of play, flutter against and brush with wings the flow
of her back. Fronds in a thousand corbeils joyously
    perfume the ground where her pads go.

And, mail uncoiling from the middle of his red
thicket of thorns, to watch above surrounding grasses,
the python rears a flat and interested head,
    but keeps his distance as she passes.

Under the towering fern she slithers out of sight
without noise. The mossed stalks bend as she shoulders by.
Sounds fall silent; the air burns; the enormous light
    sleeps on the forest and the sky.

Richmond Lattimore

THE TIGER

He paces, striped with sable and green-gold,
a nervous pendulum in a tiger cage.
The northern fog enswathes him with its cold,
blunting the snarling daggers of his rage.

He flows beneath his skin, a tropic river—
that has hurled bridges down and towns with towers
in a red maelstrom; and his nostrils quiver.
He dreams he crouches among the champak flowers.

And when the yellow moon is full his cries
(rasped from a rutting heart) evoke a mate
who crawls in sinuous bronze before blind eyes
and bluntly claws the iron bars of fate.

C. F. MacIntyre

LION

In the bend of your mouth soft murder
    in the flint of your eyes
    the sun-stained openings of caves
Your nostrils breathe the ordained air
    of chosen loneliness

Magnificently maned as the lustrous pampas
    your head heavy with heraldic curls
    wears a regal frown between the brows

The wide bundle of your chest
    your loose-skinned belly frilled with fur
    you carry easily sinuously pacing on suede paws

Between tight thighs
under the thick root of your tufted tail
situated like a full-stoned fruit beneath a bough
the quiver of your never-used malehood is slung

You pace in dung on cement
the bars flick past your eyeballs
fixed beyond the awestruck stares of children
Watching you they remember their fathers
the frightening hairs in their fathers' ears

Young girls remember lovers too timid and white
and I remember how I played lion with my brothers
under the round yellow-grained table
the shadow our cave in the lamplight

Your beauty burns the brain
though your paws slue on foul cement
the fetor of captivity you do right to ignore
the bars too an illusion

Your heroic paranoia plants you in the Indian jungle
pacing by the cool water-hole as dawn streaks the sky
and the foretaste of the all-day hunt
is sweet as yearling's blood
in the corners of your lips

May Swenson

LION

The lion is called the king
Of beasts. Nowadays there are
Almost as many lions
In cages as out of them.
If offered a crown, refuse.

Kenneth Rexroth

SONG OF THE LIONESS FOR HER CUB

Fear the one
who has sharp weapons
who wears a tassel of leopard tail,*
he who has white dogs—
O son of the short-haired lioness!
My short-eared child,
son of the lioness who devours raw flesh,
you flesh-eater!
Son of the lioness whose nostrils are red with the bleeding prey,
you with the bloodred nostrils!
Son of the lioness who drinks water from the swamp,
You water-drinker!

(*Hottentot*)

**Tassel of leopard skin*: part of the hunter's dress—a long piece of leopard skin hanging from his cap or his back.

THE LION'S SKELETON

How long, O Lion, hast thou fleshless lain?
What wrapt thy fierce and thirsty eyes away?
First came the vulture: worms, heat, wind, and rain
Ensued, and ardors of the tropic day.
I know not—if they spared it thee—how long
The canker sate within thy monstrous mane,
Till it fell piecemeal and bestrew'd the plain;
Or, shredded by the storming sands, was flung
Again to earth, but now thine ample front,

Whereon the great frowns gather'd, is laid bare;
The thunders of thy throat, which erst were wont
To scare the desert, are no longer there;
The claws remain, but worms, wind, rain, and heat
Have sifted out the substance of thy feet.

Charles Tennyson Turner

THE GREAT ALIEN

The crashed aviatrix and the startled lion
met. Loved curiously. Joined on the blond sand.

Rescued, returned to the city, the woman wept,
amputated of her peerless mate.

When she gave birth the child had tawny hair
on all his height. No tail. But a thick mane
and vigilant eyes that peered as though through bars.

He grew a comely man with great voice
used seldom except in nightmares, when he roared.

He paced the alien city, grew great with scorn.

He mined the savage city and destroyed it,
even his mother. Fled to the broad sand

to find his father, a beast magnificent,
wordless and dangerous. He slew him. Roared his grief
and stalked through night and day

and found no mate.

Dilys Laing

TIGER

A hunter cried out when he spotted a Tiger
"What a beautiful rug that creature would make!"
The Tiger growled: he did not agree;
He chased the hunter up a tree.
The hunter's gun went Bang! Bang! Bang!
Zing! Zing! Zing! the bullets sang;
A bunch of bananas plopped to the ground.
The Tiger laughed as he danced around.
He laughed so very hard, poor fellow,
Off flew his stripes of black and yellow.

When lightning flashes through the sky
And the candle glows in my cat's eye;
When thunder rolls from organ pipes,
I think I see those Tiger stripes,
I think I see them whizzing by
In streaks of lightning through the sky.

William Jay Smith

LION

The beast that is most fully dressed
Is the Lion in the yellow vest,
The velvet robes of royal red,
A crown of diamonds on his head.
His mane is combed, his paws are clean,
He looks most kingly and serene.
He rises from his royal throne
Beside his golden telephone,
And paces up and down the floor;

He groans, he growls, he starts to roar,
He roars again, he growls some more,
He tears apart his yellow vest,
He takes his robes, his diamond crown,
His telephone, and throws them down,
He kicks them all around the floor.
He gets in such a frightful rage
They have to lock him in a cage
Until he slowly quiets down
And they can give him back his crown,
His velvet robes, his yellow vest,
And he is once more fully dressed.

William Jay Smith

THE GREAT CATS AND THE BEARS

At night the great cats and the bears
Come out of all their secret lairs
To pad about with shining eyes
As planets bloom in darkened skies,
Their velvet paws as silent as
Footfall of moonlight on the grass,
And—shy explorers of our room—
So gently do they merge and loom
No one is startled, but each sense
Becomes electric in their presence.
All that they touch with magic paws
Is roused to a surprised applause,
Until upon night's inmost hour
Their fur sparks and we know their power.
The cats are roused, the bears are gay;

They take their pleasure and their play.
But what these magic ones embrace
We shall not ever know or face.
For we have fallen far below
Regions where mind can safely go.
To the primeval lairs of night
Where sense alone shines clear and bright.
And in the faint light of the dawn,
The great cats and the bears are gone.

May Sarton

EXTINCT LIONS

Where lions are extinct you will see some afternoon—
Some lion's afternoon, that is—the golden web
Of the lion's face smiling at you from an ordinary lane.
You will watch him stretch the lazy fluting of his ribs
And soar into a wall of leaves. You may not see him again.

Is it true that the lion stood like an ember in your eyes?
Or that years ago the last lion died toothless in his lair
Beyond black valleys where his skeleton still lies
Half clapsed in loam, half clasping loam in the bare
And loveless bones? You ask this, yet would you tease

The savage body forth unless with a severed will
You were thinking of the time you will break through the wall
Of leaves and into forests where extinct lions prowl,
Even as you mark time with the somnolent guile
Of passenger pigeons, cooing of the sangreal?

Radcliffe Squires

THE PANTHER

The bars he never saw: those silver lights
Of steel which weighted him like lilies. In his sight
Were children, trees, and country paths that slid
Beyond him, echoing his captiveness and hiding
Freedom from him. Visitors saw him
Safely, aptly patient, and watched that slim
Dream of self vanish in their keeping
And leave the world to sun, and, later, sleeping.

His eyes burdened him. The landscape was alive
With faces white as dolls', each one contrived
To keep its curiosity like a smile
As he crept up and down the endless mile.
Each day brought him to night again, the same
As the day before had done—each holding its lame
Tomorrow like a whispering sterile beast
Who knows its cage grows, everywhere, unceasing.

The zoo was silent in the afternoon,
Except for children. They did not mind that moon
Of blackness stationed in its ashen tree
Which made it seem that night was always there.
He slept, thick-coiled, a python in a tree.
Only a god could sleep as long as he.

Grace Carnot

THE BEAST WITHIN

I caught the lion's amber eye,
And our approaching gaze was grim;
I knew he could not leap at me;
He knew I could not leap at him.

Our eyes discoursed of liberty
Across the wide straight-sided pit.
(Yea, though the world should leap at me
Yet never dare I leap at it.)

I have a softer place to sleep
Than his; I mount a higher shelf,
There is a pit as broad and deep
Between all others and myself.

Stone jungles, deserts of cement
Hold fearful denizens and brave;
Not one has known what Nature lent
The beast within the concrete cave,

But I too pace on restless paws,
Dream of wild running on the plains
And yawning with unsated jaws
Shall leave the public my remains.

Jean Sewell Standish

ALCOHOLIC LION

I was once a believer,
But I am that no more,
Since they took me to the jungle-land
Where I heard the lion roar.

What does the lion roar with?
His head, or tail, or feet?
Or does he roar all over
When he would have his meat?

He stands outside his cavern,
To roar the whole world down.
And he roars in many a tavern
When he gets loose in town.

Kenneth Burke

ZOO

The smell assaults you first, from places
Where nightly the padded steps rehearse
Africa's movement in its restless sleep.
Here all our captive faults are nursed
Brooding in their sultry paces.

Like phrases they turn and reiterate
Lost meanings in their striped and alien cages,
Pausing to blink a heavy eye at sun
That curls up the pallid ends of pages
In their history blanked-out and done.

Now nothing remains in this sullen world
Where always on a straw-laid floor
They meditate, like prisoners in a war
Fought for lost causes, whose mere act
Of living forced them to participate.

Ignorant of ends and means, knowing
Only the blank reality of exile, they seek
The one vivid proof of life, their shadow
That alone answers when they speak—
A familiar guardian whom, a little way behind, they tow.

Watching, we turn our backs and move away,
Suddenly ashamed and moved by some glint
Of pity in their shooting eyes, as if today
They showed some symptom or some hint
Of our predicament tomorrow, or the next day.

Alan Ross

TIGER

This is the tiger god,
Weary, weary and bored;
The glowing august head
Heavy with latent fire.

The cold yellow stare
Looks into nowhere
Crossed by a steel bar—
I tremble with desire

To rouse his roar again,
To break the rigid screen;
Oh ghost in the machine
How fabulous your purr!

His heavy paws hang down;
He yawns a long slow yawn.
Never shall we be one,
I and the lambent tiger.

The whole world breaks in two
Here in the city zoo,
The bars we both look through.
Dear God, who's prisoner?

May Sarton

TIGER CUB

Tiger, of the midnight wood,
Striped in fury and in blood,
Pride thy dam and Hate thy sire,
Dreaming all thy deep desire

For prey thou shalt not kill, for dark
Pathways that never knew the mark
Of thy cruel, stealthy tread, thou thief!
Innocent captive, child of grief.

Where is the river, where the grove
Where thou shouldst wanton with thy love,
The rapturous flowers, the deep-browed kind
And lost Himalayas of thine?

Bright Inconsolable, born to rage,
Bound to the limits of thy cage.
Satan's sorrow lives in thee,
Pity's self might weep to see.

Who shall touch unhurt thy flame?
Who shall call thee by thy name?
He, thy brother and thy foe,
Shall love and never let thee go.

On a night so black and wild
He cradled thee. He came, a child,
Flesh like thee in every part
To force thy soul and break thy heart.

Martha Bacon

OCELOT

On a leash of hunger
he pulls the man
of fashion along the mall,
the black splotches
dripping smaller
near his predatory feet.
A smoky pelt
velours
the glide of his bones.

The nonchalant man
reins him in.
They pass smart windows
where stuffed facsimiles
of the cat grin
under jewelled collars.
Enough air in his bellows
to jet a leap would
choke him under the chain,

awaken a memory of crashing
wild green to devour
a wriggling snake.
Moving loosely over cement
he lunges by trees in pots
on his way to plastic bowl
on a linoleum floor.
The chain tugs. All
message to muscle is lost.

Bernice Ames

COURT OF THE LIONS: ALHAMBRA (GRANADA)

For the Monster's simplicity, the menacer's
Way to the center—what but a labyrinth?

The hieratic lions of Alhambra
Circle the court, like a map-maker's rose,
In a poodle-dog's tonsure. ferocious, solicitous,
Their muzzles, bared for the water-spout,
Four times scored with a grimace,
Their manes on their powerless shoulders, like a fleece,
Taking the basin's weight on their trumpery toes,
Among cameras, talismans, Baedekers, legendary gesso.

Only the lions keep simple.

In the labyrinth's center,
They honor a myth of the instinct's simplicity,
With a monster's indifference.
Their savage vocation,
Among pentagrams, figured cartouches, ceremonial plaster:
To humble the conjuror and mock the enchanter
With the unreflective revelation of the obvious.
The minotaur's rhetoric
And all the apparatus of the maze
Fails on their barbarous haunches
And melts in the runneling marble.

Whatever
Has blazoned the arches with calligrams, pomegranates,
eight-pointed stars,
Feathered the mortar
With the peacock's extravagance, surrenders its sorcery
Here in the lion's enclosure. Here, the invisible ring-master
That levels the hoop of the fountain's periphery
And lashes a length of cautionary water,
Would have them pigeon-breasted, plaintive, and apparent.

Yet they speak for a fable's conclusion; they prepare
For the bestial deliverer:
"The wands of the Eastern geometer
Are splintered like straw," say the lions. "The cult of the
djinn and the scarab,
The construers of entrails, wishing-bone addicts, compounders
Of formulas, philtres, phylacteries, plain and quadratic equations,
Bow the lions.
Here on the portico table,
The kingdom of nuance, the fiends of inhuman refinement,
Bend to the fallible animal. Here
The Christian intercessors of our passion,
Armed with an outcry, immediate as a stutter,
Attended by lions, strike through the net and the trident

And batter the skulls of the Arab . . ."
So say the lions:
While, on their amenable quarters,
The water falls delicate, the enchanter's enigma arises,
Plane over plane and diamond into diamond,
Bossing the surfaces, starring the grain of the panels
With the poet's *Kasidah,**
multiplying columns.

For the place of the beast is bewitched, say the lions:
The channels
Are stained with the blood of a prince's vendetta;
The thread of the fountain descends to Evangelist's navel
And charms like a hypnotist's prism.
See; even the marble devises
A sleep for the lions. Whatever their vigil,
Poem and magic are joined in a dream, for a savage's pleasure,
Alhambra assembles
Its ascending wasp-nest's heaven
Pouched in the plummeting chalks twenty ways planed
To the ceiling's improbable vertex, like a leaven;
Its columns in harvest-clusters, ringed
On the marble's shewbread; in the Mussulman script
Cursive and flourishing, repeating a violent fable
In the semblance of bowsprits, wheat-staves, cutlasses,
Hummingbird vibrations.

**Kasidah*: Arabic verse-form incorporated among the geometric and floral motifs by the Alhambra architects.

Ben Belitt

BLACK PANTHER

This little panther wears a coat of soot,
Well-suited so. Stretched out along his shelf,
Still as one brooding storm, the sultry brute
Looks soft as darkness folded on itself.

His limbs, his tarry torso, are as mat
As night wanting the stars, his resting grace
Lies leashed. Alone his head's erect: pure cat
Stares, alive with danger, in that face.

From the sharp ears down to the finest hair
At his tail's tip, he might be carved of coal.
Child of the shadows, he appears as tame,
Till, from behind the grate, the gold eyes glare
With such a light as could consume the whole
To ashes and a memory of flame.

Babette Deutsch

LIONESS ASLEEP

Content that now the bleeding bone be swept
Out of her reach, she lay upon her side.
In a blonde void sunk deep, she slept, she slept
Bland as a child, slept, breathing like a bride.
Color of noons that shimmer as they sing
Above the dunes, her sandy flanks heaved slow.
Between her paws, curled inward, billowing
Waves of desert silence seemed to flow.

The crowd was gone, the bars were gone, the cage
Thinned into air, the sawdust and the fleas
Winnowed by sleep to nothing. After food,
Absence possessed her: bliss keener than rage,
If slumber's prisoner at a bound could seize
This ghostly freedom, lapping it like blood.

Babette Deutsch

THE SNOW-LEOPARD

His pads furring the scarp's rime,
Weightless in greys and ecru, gliding
Invisibly, incuriously
As the crystals of the cirri wandering
A mile below his absent eyes,
The leopard gazes at the caravan,
The yaks groaning with tea, the burlaps
Lapping and lapping each stunned universe
That gasps like a kettle for its thinning life
Are pools in the interminable abyss
That ranges up through the ice, through air, to night.
Raiders of the unminding element,
The last cold capillaries of their kind,
They move so slowly they are motionless
To any eye less stubborn than a man's . . .
From the implacable jumble of the blocks
The grains dance icily, a scouring plume,
Into the breath, sustaining, unsustainable,
They trade to the last stillness for their death.
They sense with misunderstanding horror, with desire,
Behind the world their blood sets up in mist
The brute and geometrical necessity:
The leopard waving with a grating purr
His six-foot tail; the leopard, who looks sleepily—
Cold, fugitive, secure—at all he knows,
At all that he is: the heart of heartlessness.

Randall Jarrell

THE SPANISH LIONS

Guarding the doors of the Hispanic Society
At a Hundred and Sixty-fifth near Riverside,
Two lions sit, so charged with natural piety,

(In the Virgilian sense), so filled with pride,
They seem less carved from rock than from the spirit
Of Spain. Oh, these are lords of the Spanish law,
Castilian lions, gilt-edged and eighteen carat,
Hidalgos from rearing head to rigorous paw.

They are leaner than wasps. Yet neither thirst nor hunger
Possesses them. They thrive on honor alone,
Like granite exemplars, as if when time was younger
All lions were haughty and Spanish and made of stone.
They look down their high-bred noses. Their manes are jaunty
As a matador's queue. They stare on nothing at all—
Not even the bas-relief of Rosinante,
Posed with his Knight astride, on the opposite wall.

Phyllis McGinley

THE LION

The lion walks behind his bars,
    His tawny shoulders ebb and flow,
With swaying flank and lowered mane
    He pads the asphalt proud and slow.

If he could break his rusted cage,
    How many eyes would open wide
To see him flaring through the gap,
    A lion springing in his pride!

But now he walks with silent tread,
    Swinging and turning in his den,
He yawns and blinks his golden eyes
    Above the prying sons of men.

Herbert Asquith

LULLABY FOR AN AESOP LIONET

Little lion, single son:
all my treasures wrapped in one.
Fox and Hare are born in number
Little singlet, slumber.

Other mothers cherish more:
Two, or three, or half a score,
Wolf and Hound are born in number.
Little singlet, slumber.

Other mothers cluck at me:
such a singlet family.
Other creatures come in number.
Little Kinglet, slumber.

Norma Farber

LION IN THE NIGHT

Who wakes in the wilderness when night is done,
Fancying himself the lord of all the land,
May see what was not there at set of sun
And tremblingly will come to understand
The peril that has passed him in the dark—
Tracks of a mighty lion in the sand.

Archibald Rutledge

THE LION

The lion is a kingly beast.
He likes a Hindu for a feast.
And if no Hindu he can get,
The lion-family is upset.

He cuffs his wife and bites her ears
Till she is nearly moved to tears.
Then some explorer finds the den
And all is family peace again.

Vachel Lindsay

INDIA

They hunt, the velvet tigers in the jungle,
The spotted jungle full of shapeless patches—
Sometimes they're leaves, sometimes they're hanging flowers,
Sometimes they're hot gold patches of the sun:
They hunt, the velvet tigers in the jungle!

What do they hunt by glimmering pools of water,
By the round silver Moon, the Pool of Heaven—
In the striped grass, amid the barkless trees—
The stars scattered like eyes of beasts above them!

What do they hunt, their hot breath scorching insects,
Insects that blunder blindly in the way,
Vividly fluttering—they also are hunting,
Are glittering with a tiny ecstasy!

The grass is flaming and the trees are growing,
The very mud is gurgling in the pools,
Green toads are watching, crimson parrots flying,
Two pairs of eyes meet one another glowing—
They hunt, the velvet tigers in the jungle.

W. J. Turner

THE PANTHER

The panther is like a leopard,
Except it hasn't been peppered.
Should you behold a panther crouch,
Prepare to say Ouch.
Better yet, if called by a panther,
Don't anther.

Ogden Nash

THE LION

Oh, weep for Mr and Mrs Bryan!
He was eaten by a lion;
Following which, the lion's lioness
Up and swallowed Bryan's Bryaness.

Ogden Nash

THE CAPTIVE LION

Thou that in fury with thy knotted tail
Hast made this iron floor thy beaten drum;
That now in silence walks thy little space—
Like a sea-captain—careless what may come:

What power has brought your majesty to this,
Who gave those eyes their dull and sleepy look,
Who took their lightning out, and from thy throat,
The thunder when the whole wide forest shook?

It was that man who went again, alone,
Into thy forest dark—Lord, he was brave!
That man a fly has killed, whose bones are left
Unburied till an earthquake digs his grave.

W. H. Davies

INCIDENT WITH LIONS

Into the Arc, by docile two and seven,
The obedient animals filed.
But there were some, I think, too proud, too wild
Thus to be herded and driven.
Lions, surely, who shook the night with thunder
There on the last hill,
Drenched and bedraggled and doomed, but imperial still,
Watching the world go under.
Noah had trouble finding some of that kin
Whom he could hustle aboard.
At bay, the princely lions paced and roared
And would not save their skin.
They stood while the heavens split and the flood rolled
And chose to drown deep
To the company of jackal and rat and the witless sheep
In the Ark's stinking hold.

Sara Henderson Hay

THE TIGRESS

The raging and the ravenous,
The nocturnal terror in gold,
Red-fire-coated, green-fire-eyed,
The fanged, the clawed, the frightful leaper.

Wild

Great-sinewed, silent walker,
Tyrant of all the timid, the implacable
Devil of slaughter, the she-demon
Matchless in fury, matchless love
Gives her whelps in the wilderness.
Gleaning the smears of slaughter
From her jaws with tongue and forearm,
She licks her young and suckles them
Delicately as a doe:
She blood-glutted is the angel
To their blindness, she is minister
Between life and these feeble young
In barren places, where no help is.

Or man-imprisoned often disdaining
To rear her royal brood, though cheated
Into bearing, she abandons
All at birth, and bids them die.
Utter love and utter hatred
Cannot compromise: she gives
Her whole being to their being
Or rejects them into death.

No thought intervenes, her justice
Is not mind-perverted: O tigress,
Royal mother without pity.
Could but one thought arise within
That greatly sculptured skull, behind
Those phosphorous eyes compunction burn.
Well might it be a thought for many
Men through the mother mind-betrayed,
No beast so hapless as a man.

Ruth Pitter

THE JAGUAR

The apes yawn and adore their fleas in the sun.
The parrots shriek as if they were on fire, or strut
Like cheap tarts to attract the stroller with the nut.
Fatigued with indolence, tiger and lion

Lie still as the sun. The boa-constrictor's coil
Is a fossil. Cage after cage seems empty, or
Stinks of sleepers from the breathing straw.
It might be painted on a nursery wall.

But who runs like the rest past these arrives
At a cage where the crowd stands, stares, mesmerized,
As a child at a dream, at a jaguar hurrying enraged
Through prison darkness after the drills of his eyes

On a short fierce fuse. Not in boredom—
The eye satisfied to be blind in fire,
By the bang of blood in the brain deaf the ear—
He spins from the bars, but there's no cage to him

More than to the visionary his cell:
His stride is wildernesses of freedom:
The world rolls under the long thrust of his heel.
Over the cage floor the horizons come.

Ted Hughes

AT THE LION CAGE

The air takes gold from his shower of mane,
a regal mark; held in his amber gaze
horizons dwindle to a minute size
from which, a royal prisoner of man,
he makes an exit through his captor's eyes.

Oliver Hale

THE LION IN THE WILLOW

In the tangle of yellow,
in the cage of the mane if only
the fangs would flash,
I'd be sure, sure
of my sovereign terror.

Beastly he lurks in his maze,
silent, captive,
his hair in his hotsummer eyes,
his leonine burrow gold-burgeoned
with leaves that snarl him offguard.

Padded in skeins, his claws
pussyfoot like secrets.
I'll find him, I'll find him,
I'll follow him deep and plumb
to the ravel of frost.

I'll know him in molt,
in the shed of his mask,
in the bland of his fierce renown,
his hirsute dazzle a kitten,
a sun come winter.

Norma Farber

LOOK YOU'RE LAUGHING

Look you're laughing when we point out the prints
the cougar made, the mark of each paw
preserved in fresh snow . . . The four firm
toes are spread no wider than my palm.
Yet you can almost feel the force
of her high flanks and chest that pressed them so.

Desperate in winter, driven by hunger, the female
snuck into camp at dusk, sniffing the smoke,
pretending to be about other business
as she took a bed roll by one stray corner
between her teeth, shook it, let it go
and leaped away on the long white slope

the blur of her brown and rust colored coat in the mind
of everyone talking at once, telling what you missed.
Look you're laughing but if you saw the cat
creeping over to pull at your pillow
then we could show other people the shallow tracks
you left behind, your feet hardly even touching the snow.

George Keithley

LION-TAMING-ACT

With a great cracking of whips, the lady
    enters
And, One-Two-Three-Four-Five—
A pause and a snarl—then, Six, the great
    beasts shoulder
Into the cage beside her. (Any one
Could eat her alive.)
And we in the circus crowd pull a breath
    quick with terror.
Inside with her—yet out, with the bars
Neatly persuaded between ourselves and
    disaster—
But the fear she embraces is really partly
    ours,
And ours the pride as, Crack-crack-crack!
    though they threaten,
Whip-trained, with a massive precision,

Six lions have leaped upon stools,
And the lady is bowing in triumph,
The great beasts submissive and cowed.
Each hunched on his stool like a schoolboy—
She drinks the applause of the crowd.

And if, some unusual night, the
    whip-cracking lady
Had flicked too sharply at something
    beneath the fur
Of one of the cowering sullen beaten lions,
So that, instead of retreating, it leaped
    on *her*,
Why, wouldn't it make a nice surprise for
    the lady?
Tending, as I think it would, to prove
That though you may profit by terror,
It's a trifle more risky than love.

Frances Minturn Howard

STALKED

When I go to see the lions,
it is already dusk.
I lean on the wall and watch
the untamed ballet on the rocky slope.

A large male raises his head
and looks at me
with a look I have seen before.
The watcher becomes the watched.

The lion advances, crouches,
never shifting his yellow eyes.
The other visitors have gone,
and the wind is cold.

I came for casual pleasure;
now he wants dinner.
We are both predators,
feeling neither cruel nor compassionate.

He has already clawed me with my guilt,
stripped off the skin and
tossed it to me.
How far will justice go today?

He leaps into the moat
directly below me.
I hear him growl in his throat
like a dog who means it.

His claws slide on the wall.
Half-testing,
I move toward the other end, toward escape.
His pads keep pace.

Jerene Cline

SNOW LEOPARD

There comes a chalk awakening;
the spotted sleeper stalks—
his image of hunger
barred and screened and blocked;
grey in his grace, and leaping—
a leopard leaving us glad
for capture and for keeping
the paw that was endowed,
native, with fury's power.
But here his ruthless cunning,
absurdum, is reduced,
caged, to a kitten's clowning.
And he is served his blood

then licks, a docile carnivore,
a craving curled and fed—
He purrs like satisfaction,
looks possible to pet—
our hope for snow abstraction:
death's leopard looking out.

Harold Witt

TO SPEAK TO A LION

I wouldn't know how to speak
to a lion
had I never communed
with a cat.
This startling discovery
came about
with a complete absence
of thought.

A great idea must arrive
by itself—
from no one should it
be rifled:
if once you have conversed
with a cat
all lions will remain unruffled.

Jean Harper

CAPTIVE LIONS

"As these lordly animals pace restlessly up and down, visitors may wonder if they are thinking of their far-off home in the desert or jungle. As a matter of fact, most captive lions now in zoos probably never saw the lands of their ancestors. They breed well in captivity, and most captive lions were born in zoos."

—*The World Book.*

I was about to write about
zoo lions sad for home,
stretched out on artificial rock
who dozing seem to dream

of freedom's sun-maned Africa,
but looking *lions* up
I read that most were zoo born
and easily adjust.

Behind the moat and bars
in a landscape hosed of dust,
they've rolled and hissed their whiskers
since they were spotted cubs,

and climbed the simulated trees
and slept upon concrete
and shot out paws of power
at what's shoved underneath.

Grandiose of grace,
in attitudes of sphinx,
captive lions, gazing,
aren't as the viewer thinks,

more than any cat is,
grieving to go back—
they're livelier with what they have
than dying from a lack,

more fertile than in nature
(they feel what leisure's for),
with greater manes and better teeth
and a gold gloss to their fur—

there may be something on the side
of living in a cage,
especially if you're a lion
on a printed page.

Harold Witt

THE FISHER CAT

Wildness sleeps upon the mountain
And then it wakes in an animal
And in us, and in the sophistication of city streets
And in the danger of the indifferent murder,
We see the fisher cat on the limb of the tree.
Or is it a marten, or what is this slim, fierce beast
Caught in the flashlight's glare at night in Vermont,
Ready to leap at the baying dogs?

This enemy, this ancient foe, what is he?
The unexpected beast glares down from the high branch
Ready to pounce and fills man with fear,
Some nameless fear of millions of years ago in the forest,
Or the Rift valley in East Africa
When it was life or death in an instant.

The man has a gun, the instrument that has saved him,
Without which the drama of this intense moment
Might have ended in the death of man, and no poem;
He raised his piece like a violator of nature
And aiming at the jewelled caskets of the eyes
Brought the treasure trove of brain and sport.

The beast fell to the ground, unable to comment,
His beauty despoiled that took millions of years to grow.
The dogs thrashed around a while and quieted.
The New England hunter then with his matter of fact,
Taking for granted his situation mastery, put the
Mythic beast in the back of his four wheel drive vehicle.

It has taken the scientists of the university months
To decide what kind of an animal the creature was.
The centimeters of the back molars were counted,
Books were consulted, in the end it was decided,
Not by the scientist but by the poet, that a god
Had descended on man, and had to be killed.

Wildness sleeps upon the mountain
And when it wakes in us,
There is a moment, perilous of stasis
When savagery meets equal savagery.
The long arm of man maintains intelligence
By death: his gun rang out instant doom.
The paws of the animal were very wide,
The claws of the beast were wide, long his thrashing tail.

Richard Eberhart

HONEY FROM THE LION

I came upon it unaware . . .
But there was sand and silence there,
Blue-burning haze and scorching rock,
Short-daggered grass . . . and then the shock
Of great limbs stretched before a lair:

The old brave body still and prone,
Of some king-lion done to death
Upon the threshold of his earth,
All that huge ardor still as stone.

Wild bees had built their honeycomb
In his bright carcass, thunder-maned.
Through brow and jaw the nectar strained:
What Pharaoh in his spicy tomb
Had such rich amber seal his mouth?

I dipped my fingers in the sweet
And oh! the fiery savage meat
Bred from the lands of lack and drouth,
Tanged with wild joy and deep unrest
And desolate courage and the strength
Of loneliness: I knew at length
What fury burned in Samson's breast!

Now garden honey's overmild
To satisfy the sharpened taste
Of one who's eaten of the waste.
I know a hunger never filled
Since that strange banquet long ago,
That dark and bitter sweetness grown
Out of the lion's blood and bone,
Out of the desert's pride and woe.

Leah Bodine Drake

WILDCAT

A wildcat lurks behind this hillside town;
His golden eyes are flowers in the dark
And stripes run from the trees into his fur,
Furrowed like piney-bark in black and brown.
How big he is, no one can rightly say—
But big enough to frighten and delight;
And like a wild rose vine his thorny track

Is found long after he has gone away.
His boundaries are altered by his will;
The town seems wider while the cat's at large
Within a necessary wilderness
And we remember there remains a hill
No man has walked on yet. We let him range
The province of our willful ignorance,
Above geraniumed streets, out of our sight,
Dark disarranger of our dreams at night.

Frances Colvin

BUSH

It is the sound of lions lapping.
They drink themselves
from the gold shapes that waver
and grow shallower.

Blue peels itself in the water-
hole: it is the sun coming.
Crouched, the lions meet
their matches at the surface.

The foxy jackals are far off
but the vultures cloud the flat treetop;
the drum of the zebra's body
is lined with red sunrise.

The jackals and vultures are waiting
for what happened under the moon.
The lions are through with it; they
lift their dripping chins and look ahead.

Wild

It is six o'clock on Christmas morning.
Now the lions have stopped lapping
the bush makes no sound
the vultures shift, but without sound.

The day is perfectly seamless.
Slowly the lions move like pistons past the dry grasses;
the jackals do not move yet;
the vultures show patience.

The lions pass a thornbush and melt.
Though the whole day is unbroken
the passage of the sun will represent heaven;
the bones will represent time.

Josephine Jacobsen

6.

UNDEFINED

AND I WILL CONSIDER MY CAT CAITLIN

Twanged through Cat Heaven the utmost toughest thread
Of nine car-dodging lives but never snapped.
Eight knocked out, the last one nearly dead,
She limped bloodily home from the grave's edge of the road.
You, so easily suggesting the mercy shot,
Consider my cat Caitlin clean as a swan shift,
Lying in her own ordure, the long dirty agony of the ditch.
And I will praise Christopher Smart, and the vet,
Setting her broken jaw and one leg, as I listen now
To the terrible sound of her unsheathed claws
On the window ledge, through my lulled house
The frightful miaow's beware to the mousey wainscot
Of eight lives risen from the dead.

Eric Barker

CAT BALLERINA ASSOLUTA

The white cat
    Light paws about the studio,
Dances cloudsome among Madam's pupils
    Aching, stretching at the *barre*,
Mocks them with her *pas de chats*,
Teases with her *en l'air*,
Down stares them with her lemon drop eyes

Is Madam a spit-spite,
    A catty teacher?
Showing up her groundlings,
Sly dealing them a puss
    Who leaps with a *ballon* beyond them
For ribbons they try to bind round taffy ankles,
She neat points a pop pearl,

Jetés a lost earring,
Such batterie, *battement,*
The *pas de bourrées, the entrechats*
Prima without pulled ligaments,
Assòluta without sweat, slipped discs,
Prima ballerina assoluta,
They claw her with their glances

White cat
White as a tutu,
White cat with the lemon drop eyes,
Upstaging
She earths them with every *jeté*
Needs no massage, no practice *barre,*
They soil their toe shoes in slopping tries
While her paws white point,
They can flex and stretch, strain and sprain,
And never be a white cat dancing

White demon
Pavlova cat,
You think the world owes you a living,
You hunger strike for delicacies,
Must you *prima* about
Belittling Madam's pupils?
You cat you
Cat

Emilie Glen

OLD TOM

An old, black, rutting tomcat,
The brother of his female,
Expressed nature in his sister
Begetting again his future.

I eye this old, mangy fellow
With a certain sympathy.
His progeny already
Have suffered fortune and misfortune

Teaching us, as larger animals,
Something of ourselves.
As poets will to survive,
Cats survive by force.

A kitten could not be expected
To understand a moving car.
One, atop my front wheel,
Was rolled down to mutilation.

I had to kill her with a club
And buried her in the bushes,
Shaking with the dread of this
But doing it nevertheless.

Her little brother very soon
Had caught a bird so beautiful
I hated to see it mutilated,
And left only feathers and the spleen.

They are the most civilized creatures,
Sleep all day and hunt by night,
Elegance in the drawing room,
Merciless in dusk or in moonlight.

But most it is their indifference
To death of their own fellows
I applaud; they go about their business,
Unquestioning the fates of those fellows.

Old Tom, here is a handout,
Some meal and some milk for you.
Go rough it under the stars,
You teach us what we are

When our policies are riven
And our pretentions are bare,
And we are subservient to nature
Very much as you are.

Richard Eberhart

THE RETIRED CAT

A Poet's cat, sedate and grave,
As poet well could wish to have,
Was much addicted to inquire
For nooks, to which she might retire,
And where, secure as mouse in chink,
She might repose, or sit and think.
I know not where she caught the trick—
Nature perhaps herself had cast her
In such a mould *philisophique,*
Or else she learned it of her master.
Sometimes ascending, debonair,
An apple-tree or lofty pear,
Lodg'd with convenience in the fork,
She watched the gard'ner at his work;
Sometimes her ease and solace sought
In an old empty wat'ring pot,
There wanting nothing, save a fan,
To seem some nymph in her sedan,
Apparelled in exactest sort,
And ready to be borne to court.
    But love of change it seems has place
Not only in our wiser race;
Cats also feel as well as we
That passion's force, and so did she.
Her climbing, she began to find,
Exposed her too much to the wind,

And the old utensil of tin
Was cold and comfortless within:
She therefore wished instead of those,
Some place of more serene repose,
Where neither cold might come, nor air
Too rudely wanton with her hair,
And sought it in the likeliest mode
Within her master's snug abode.
    A drawer,—it chanced, at bottom lined
With linen of the softest kind,
With such as merchants introduce
From India, for the ladies' use,—
A drawer impending o'er the rest,
Half open in the topmost chest,
Of depth enough, and none to spare,
Invited her to slumber there.
Puss with delight beyond expression,
Surveyed the scene, and took possession.
Recumbent at her ease ere long,
And lulled by her own hum-drum song,
She left the cares of life behind,
And slept as she would sleep her last,
When in came, housewifely inclined,
The chambermaid, and shut it fast,
By no malignity impelled,
But all unconscious whom it held.
    Awakened by the shock (cried puss)
Was ever cat attended thus!
The open drawer was left, I see,
Merely to prove a nest for me,
For soon as I was well composed,
Then came the maid, and it was closed:
How smooth these kerchiefs, and how sweet,
O what a delicate retreat!
I will resign myself to rest
Till Sol, declining in the west,
Shall call to supper; when, no doubt,

Susan will come and let me out.
    The evening came, the sun descended,
And puss remained still unattended.
The night rolled tardily away,
(With her indeed 'twas never day)
The sprightly morn her course renewed,
The evening gray again ensued,
And puss came into mind no more
Than if entombed the day before.
With hunger pinched, and pinched for room,
She now presaged approaching doom,
Nor slept a single wink, or purred,
Conscious of jeopardy incurred.
    That night, by chance, the poet watching,
Heard an inexplicable scratching,
His noble heart went pit-a-pat,
And to himself he said—what's that?
He drew a curtain at his side,
And forth he peeped, but nothing spied.
Yet, by his ear directed, guessed
Something imprisoned in the chest,
And doubted what, with prudent care,
Resolved it should continue there.
At length a voice, which he well knew,
A long and melancholy mew,
Saluting his poetic ears,
Consoled him, and dispelled his fears;
He left his bed, he trod the floor,
He 'gan in haste the drawers explore,
The lowest first, and without stop,
The rest in order to the top.
For 'tis a truth well known to most,
That whatsoever thing is lost,
We seek it, ere it come to light,
In every cranny but the right.
Forth skipped the cat; not now replete
As erst with airy self-conceit,

Nor in her own fond apprehension,
A theme for all the world's attention,
But modest, sober, cured of all
Her notions hyberbolical,
And wishing for a place to rest
Anything rather than a chest;
Then stepped the poet into bed,
With this reflection in his head:

MORAL

Beware of too sublime a sense
Of your own worth and consequence!
The man who dreams himself so great,
And his importance of such weight,
That all around, in all that's done,
Must move and act for him alone,
Will learn, in school of tribulation,
The folly of his expectation.

William Cowper

ODE ON THE DEATH OF A FAVORITE CAT, DROWNED IN A TUB OF GOLD FISHES

'Twas on a lofty vase's side,
Where China's gayest art had dy'd
The azure flowers that blow;
Demurest of the tabby kind,
The pensive Selima reclin'd,
Gazed on the lake below.

Her conscious tail her joy declar'd;
The fair round face, the snowy beard,
The velvet of her paws,
Her coat, that with the tortoise vies,
Her ears of jet, and emerald eyes,
She saw; and purr'd applause.

Still had she gaz'd; but 'midst the tide
Two angel forms were seen to glide,
    The Genii of the stream:
Their scaly armour's Tyrian hue
Thro' richest purple to the view
    Betray'd a golden gleam.

The hapless Nymph with wonder saw:
A whisker first and then a claw,
    With many an ardent wish,
She stretch'd in vain to reach the prize,
What female heart can gold despise?
    What Cat's averse to fish?
Presumptuous Maid! with looks intent
Again she stretch'd, again she bent,
    Nor knew the gulf between.
(Malignant Fate sat by, and smil'd)
The slipp'ry verge her feet beguil'd.
    She tumbled headlong in.

Eight times emerging from the flood
She mew'd to ev're watry God,
    Some speedy aid to send.
No Dolphin came, no Nereid stirr'd:
Nor cruel *Tom*, nor *Susan* heard.
    A Fav'rite has no friend!

From hence, ye Beauties, undeceiv'd,
Know, one false step is ne'er retriev'd,
    And be with caution bold.
Not all that tempts your wand'ring eyes
And heedless hearts, is lawful prize;
    Nor all that glisters, gold.

Thomas Gray

THE FORUM ON FRIDAY

At sunset, from
across the Senate steps
behind horizontal pillars
through emblazoned arches
around fragmented torsos
in the waning gold light
among breathing flowers
sprouting grass, birds, shadows—
to look at fallen kings
and lick their paws—
cats come.

Daisy Stieber Squadra

THE CAT AND THE MISER

Nothing could have brought him to the door,
This brown, this dripping night,
But the faint noise that did: a plucking,
Plucking at the tight
Copper crosswires of the screen.

He knew. It was the cat.
Her signal to come in.
Or thought he knew, the miser,
As with a groan, a sly grin,
Shuffling, he slid the bolt.

No eyes would have been so welcome,
Staring up and blinking.
But these, the tall thief's—
Oh, oh! the unthinking
Blow, the heavy feet.

Oh, oh! The boxes gone,
The misery. Then here she was:
Pluck, pluck—the sound,
In and out, of delicate claws.
What fiend had listened?

Out there, what sharpened face,
Vigilant, had learned the trick?
He staggered up and let her through.
Late, late! A sudden kick—
But then, caresses.

Mark Van Doren

CATS AND KINGS

With wide unblinking stare
The cat looked; but she did not see the king—
She only saw a two-legged creature there
Who, in due time, might have tit-bits to fling.

The king was on his throne.
In his left hand he grasped a golden ball.
She looked at him with eyes of bright green stone
And thought, *What fun if he should let it fall.*

With swishing tail she lay
And watched for happy accidents, while he,
The essential king, was brooding far away
In his own world with hope and memory.

O, cats are subtle now,
And kings are mice to many a modern mind.
And yet there throbbed behind the human brow
The strangely simple thoughts that serve mankind.

The gulf might not be wide;
But over it, at least, no cat could spring.
So once again an ancient adage lied.
The cat looked, but she never saw the king.

Alfred Noyes

THE PETS

Colm had a cat,
and a wren,
and a fly.

The cat was a pet,
and the wren,
and a fly.

And it happened that the wren
ate the fly;
and it happened that the cat
ate the wren.

Then the cat died.

So Saint Colm lacked a cat
and a wren,
and a fly.

But Saint Colm loved the cat,
and the wren,
and a fly,

so he prayed to get them back,
cat and wren;
and he prayed to get them back,
wren and fly.

And the cat became alive
and delivered up the wren;
and the wren became alive
and delivered up the fly;
and they all lived with Colm
till the day came to die.

First the cat died.
Then the wren died.
Then the fly.

Robert Farren

THE CAT AND THE BIRD

Tell me, tell me, gentle Robin,
What is it sets thy heart a-throbbing?
Is it that Grimalkin fell
Hath killed thy father or thy mother,
Thy sister or thy brother,
Or any other?
Tell me that,
And I'll kill the Cat.

But stay, little Robin, did you ever spare
A grub on the ground or a fly in the air?
No, that you never did, I'll swear;
So I won't kill the Cat,
That's flat.

George Canning

POEM

As the cat
climbed over
the top of

the jamcloset
first the right
forefoot

carefully
then the hind
stepped down

into the pit of
the empty
flower pot

William Carlos Williams

TWO SONGS OF A FOOL

I

A speckled cat and a tame hare
Eat at my hearthstone
And sleep there;
And both look up to me alone
For learning and defence
As I look up to Providence.

I start out of my sleep to think
Some day I may forget
Their food and drink;
Or, the house door left unshut,
The hare may run till it's found
The horn's sweet note and the tooth of the hound.

I bear a burden that might well try
Men that do all by rule,
And what can I
That am a wandering-witted fool
But pray to God that He ease
My great responsibilities.

II

I slept on my three-legged stool by the fire,
The speckled cat slept on my knee;
We never thought to enquire
Where the brown hare might be,
And whether the door were shut.
Who knows how she drank the wind
Stretched up on two legs from the mat,
Before she had settled her mind
To drum with her heel and to leap?
Had I but awakened from sleep
And called her name, she had heard,
It may be, and had not stirred,
That now, it may be, has found
The horn's sweet note and the tooth of the hound.

William Butler Yeats

THERE WAS A WEE BIT MOUSIKIE

There was a wee bit mousikie,
    That lived in Bilberary-O,
It couldno' get a bite o'cheese,
    For Cheatie-Pussy-Catty-O.

It said unto the cheesity,
    "Oh fain would I be at ye-O
If 'Twere not' for the cruel claws
    O' Cheatie-Pussy-Catty-O."

Anon.

CAT

My cat
Is quiet
She moves without a sound.
Sometimes she stretches herself curving
On tiptoe.
Sometimes she crouches low
And creeping.

Sometimes she rubs herself against a chair,
And there
    With a *miew* and a *miew*
    And a purrr purrr purrr
    She curls up
    And goes to sleep.

My cat
Lives through a black hole
Under the house
So one day I
Crawled in after her
And it was dark
And I sat
And didn't know
Where to go.
And then—

Two yellow-white
Round little lights
Came moving . . . moving . . . toward me
And there
With a *miew* and a *miew*
And a purrr   purrr   purrr
My cat
Rubbed, soft, against me.

And I knew
The lights
Were MY CAT'S EYES
In the dark.

Dorothy Baruch

CAT

The black cat yawns,
Opens her jaws,
Stretches her legs,
And shows her claws.

Then she gets up
and stands on four
Long stiff legs
And yawns some more.

She shows her sharp teeth,
She stretches her lip,
Her slice of a tongue
Turns up at the tip.

Lifting herself
On her delicate toes,
She arches her back
As high as it goes.

She lets herself down
With particular care,
And pads away
With her tail in the air.

Mary Britton Miller

CAT ON A HOLIDAY

He is a paw-swarm crossing the railroad tracks
To a warehouse and siding, where he scouts
His outworks for the thin parings of daily existence.
Daily the boxcars visit, and bring him
The scents of plenty from far places
He has never been to (Florida he knows
By the fragrance of oranges, Oregon
From its lumber aromas): his only world
Is the warehouse, his plenty the warehouse marauders.
Elsewhere, outside his world, today thanks are given
And feasts spread; but he fasts at locked doors
And over odors at the cellar gratings; squats waiting
For the day after, his body grown used to
Its never-enough; mouths a nut, shelters
Among Christmas firs for tomorrow's wholesaling;
And under the warehouse graffiti of PEACE
And LOVE sits grinning, a joke without laughter.

Nancy G. Westerfield

IN A HOTEL LOBBY

Nowhere in five weeks of travel
had I seen one until, there at last,
asleep on the red carpet of the
hotel lobby
beneath an unlit lamp,

sprawled black,
panther-huge
(why not in a land of shrimps
and cheeses?)
white paw curved relaxed
along a gold claw of the lamp base . . .
Wake up, I willed.

Eyes opened in a half-mooned blaze of light
both sinister and benign,
and closed again.
A voice shrilled behind me. "What *are* you
doing on the floor behind that chair?"

How could I explain something self-contained,
secure, complete, beyond a fact?
I rose to my feet, unfolded, expanded,
smiling to myself.
"I just took my last picture on my last film—
an Amsterdam cat."

Hortense Roberta Roberts

CHARLIE'S LEGS

Charlie's legs
are brown

& his lips
& eyelashes

Undefined

Charlie's legs
support ten
brown cat pounds

Charlie's legs
walk under
yellow eyes

pupils running
north to south

he lays his
legs down
side by side

in their old
brown velvet

he often lays
his brown legs
down

& his lips
& eyelashes

Eleanor B. Zimmerman

CATS

I declare dependence: your vigils and
      visits
bring weather indoors, your pelts and
      paws
are scented with morning and evening.

You assume incorruptible indifference
or assault me with timed, untimely
attentions;
hide pencils, crouch on my open book—
to suggest the error of sublimation,
to substitute word with look?
You command the hand to touch, exalt
the tactile.
Your coats are vari-colored, deep,
sleekly my palm fits your skulls.

You exhibit perfections of sleep.

You have taught me the nuance of four-
footed dances.
You tense with attention to pleasure,
to all that flickers and trails; sun-patches,
string
or those constant things begging for
capture,
your own tip-twitching tails.

Your loves are violent, vocal, regretting
nothing
and guilt has no dominion, you do not
sigh.
You are curious about, not critical of—
unquestioned under your round gem-eyes
man and I may enact our unseasonal
love.

Joanne de Longchamps

IN CONNECTICUT THERE ARE CATS

In Connecticut there are cats
Sitting on white porches, prowling
Through dandelions, sleeping
On sunny window seats. Sturdy
Yankee cats in Connecticut
Are black or white or orange
Striped with short practical coats
Battle scarred in brief domestic wars.
Connecticut cats care little
For dogs or men as they wash
Their fine morning faces, eschew
Synthetic city food for country
Cream and watch the New England
Spring come up the road as easily
As a cat himself. Redbud, dogwood,
Apple blossom take precedent
For an hour and then move on.
Connecticut cats have seen Springs come
And go. Window seats endure.

Betty Lowry

ON DINO, MY CAT, WHO FLEW ACROSS THE CONTINENT

Dino, arranged in a purr,
Having already arrived
Before starting,
Shows only unbemused fur
While flying, tranquilized,
To me.

Waiting, arranged in a whirl,
Not having arrived
In many a frantic beginning,
I am that kind of girl
Who needs visitation of
Such kind.

Karen Rose

HODGE AND DOCTOR JOHNSON

Poor Hodge, the cat, fell ailing,
his appetite had gone;
no tidbit in the larder
could tempt his fevered tongue.

It was an anxious morning
in Doctor Johnson's house
when Hodge who guarded learning
lost interest in a mouse.

Might Frank, perhaps, the houseboy—
yet humble folk could fret
should Doctor Johnson send them
on errands for a pet.

Miss Williams, she was sightless,
and Levet tippled wine.
A fig, mused the Carmichael,
what if poor Hodge should pine.

Though lords in lace might tremble
at Doctor Johnson's rage,
though fops and fools took cover,
he was a gentle sage.

So out strode Doctor Johnson,
that Dictionary great,
that man of grace and thunder,
rotund, with seaman's gait.

Then off the caps came doffing
as the great man rolled along—
no larger mind that morning
heard the oyster wench's song.

Till home he came, prize-laden,
a packet on his arm
of succulent sweet oysters
poor Hodge's heart to warm.—

Keen scholar, wise with Plutarch,
with Boswell very wise,
who taught to hunt in trifles
a great man's qualities.

Sarah Wingate Taylor

SEA CATS AT DUSK

At six o'clock the boats come in,
At six o'clock the cats come down—
The Harbor Street Irregulars,
The highwaymen who haunt the town
Report for duty. Weathered piers
Are crowned with furry ornament,
Heads high, tails furled. They stare and stare
And sniff for news of fish. They sent
Their blessings with the boats at dawn,
And now the wise but weary crews,
Grumbling at the blackmailers,
Toss out the tribute, pay their dues.

Bianca Bradbury

PULLMAN CAT

I never purchased the ticket, his silence says:
I never ordered this move. Aloof,
He shows me his humped hindside on the bed;
Or morose, sits and stares from the window
At a snowing, kaleidoscope world. The ears point forward
For nothing familiar; he scorns
The food brought in white-coated style
To his door from the diner; scorns drink,
Scorns love, scorns all my apology:
He uncurls a tongue like an anchovy and yawns,
Only warily trusting me and the berth, curls
On himself smelling wheaten and sunny, and sleeps.

Nancy G. Westerfield

UNQUESTIONABLY CAT

The orange cat
runs twice at once:
on the fence and on
the snow's calm mirror.
He doesn't ask the cedar
fence how long it's
watched the yard. Watched
the birds and squirrels,
snowflakes, leaves and rain-
drops. Nor does he ask
the mirror who
is fairest of the fair.
What cat
would ask this question?
He knows he is himself.
And there.

A. D. Freeman

CAMERA STUDY

In the town of Bourton-on-the-Water
(the Venice of the Cotswolds),
by the Windrush River,
a white
tomcat
dozed on the high circle
of a fence pole,
folded within himself like a pillow.
Hearing me stalk him
through the jungle of his dream,
he slowly stretched alive,
and posed,
tall as a jug of cream,
one paw lifted to salute or shrive,
as I clicked
clicked
clicked
hello.

Jean Burden

WALKING WITH LULU IN THE WOOD

The wood is a good place to find
the other road down to that hollow
which rocks a little with the same
motion as my soul. Come on, Lulu,
follow me and be careful of the rain
washed leaves. But you were always gentle.
I'll be quiet too, and we won't disturb
the raccoons or any of the other animals.
I want to talk with the god here, Lulu.
This is a grove where he must be hiding,
and here is a pool for a small water god
to swim in. Let's talk with the god, Lulu.

The sun makes a great splash and you
are the one who is hiding in the tall grass
just the way you used to. Lulu,
you are the color of sand in a certain light,
like the shadow of light. The sun
is embracing me; the shadow also
means death. It is the god's word
in the language he speaks. He says
you are small again, that you have chosen it.
He says your reflection will be in the pool
forever, a blue resemblance, a startled joy.
He says this is your world now, this night
of tall trees, this cave of silences.
He says he loves you too; he watches you sleep.

Is the grove real? Is this your heaven, Lulu,
that you have let me enter? This glade,
the winter ivories?—the season you missed
by dying in the fall. Are these your jewelled
stones, your curled-up animals, your grass?
And your god, the secret splash in the water
that you always seemed to be listening for?
Is it the god's way—the mouth in the wood,
the opening to paradise?

God of animals and children, separations, loss.
Goodbye. Goodbye, sweet girl, again.
The days pass like oranges tossed
from hand to hand. Then one will drop
and it will be my turn. Wait for me here.
I hope to be fortunate, to come back and share
this winter wood with you, the dark hollow,
the snow-dusted face of the god.

Naomi Lazard

ACKNOWLEDGEMENTS

Abelard-Schuman Limited: "The Cat!" by Joseph Payne Brennan, from *Halloween Through Twenty Centuries,* compiled by Ralph and Adelin Linton, copyright © 1950 by Henry Schuman, Inc., by permission of Abelard-Schuman Limited, an Intext publisher.

Accent: "The Panther" by Grace Carnot, Winter 1955. Accent is no longcr published.

George Allen & Unwin Ltd.: "Cat" from *The Adventures of Tom Bombadil* by J. R. R. Tolkien, Canadian rights only, courtesy of George Allen & Unwin.

Ashland Poetry Press: "If Black " from *Now, Swim,* by Harold Witt, copyright © 1974 by Harold Witt, by permission of the author.

William L. Bauhan, publisher: "Remembered Cat" from *Collected Poems, 1932–1961,* by George Abbe, copyright © 1961 by George Abbe, by permission of William L. Bauhan.

Ben Belitt: "Court of the Lions: Alhambra" from *The Enemy Joy,* published by the University of Chicago Press, copyright © 1964 by Ben Belitt, by permission of the author to whom rights have reverted.

The Bodley Head Ltd.: "Diamond Cut Diamond" from *Diamond Cut Diamond,* by Ewart Milne, 1950, by permission of The Bodley Head Ltd.

R. L. Bryan Company: "Lion in the Night" from *Deep River: Complete Poems of Archibald Rutledge,* copyright © 1960 by R. L. Bryan Company, by permission of R. L. Bryan Company.

Cambridge University Press: "Song of the Lioness for Her Cub" from *African Poetry,* compiled and edited by Ulli Beier, copyright © 1966 Cambridge University Press, by permission of Cambridge University Press.

Chatto and Windus, Ltd.: "Concord Cats" from *Collected Poems* by Richard Eberhart, Canadian rights only, courtesy of the author and Chatto and Windus.

The Christian Science Monitor: "Cat on the porch at Dusk" by Dorothy Harriman, published September 17, 1952; and "Lullaby for an Aesop Lionet" by Norma Farber, published August 4, 1959, reprinted by permission from The Christian Science Monitor, copyright © 1952 and 1959, respectively, The Christian Science Publishing Society. All rights reserved.

Collins-Knowlton-Wing, Inc.: "Cat Goddesses" from *Collected Poems* by Robert Graves, published by Doubleday & Company, copyright © 1958, 1961 by Robert Graves. Reprinted by permission of Collins-Knowlton-Wing, Inc., agents for Mr. Graves.

Commonweal Publishing Co., Inc.: "Wildcat" by Frances Colvin, published December 17, 1965, copyright © 1965 by Commonweal, by permission of Commonweal Publishing Co., Inc.

Coward, McCann & Geoghegan, Inc.: "Cats and Zinnias" from *CATS in Prose and Verse*, by Nelson Antrim Crawford, copyright © 1947 by Nelson Antrim Crawford; "Tiger Cub" from *Things Visible and Invisible* by Martha Bacon, copyright © 1947 by Martha Bacon. Both poems reprinted by permission of Coward, McCann & Geoghegan, Inc.

Mrs. Jibanananda Das: "Cat" by Jibanananda Das, translated by Lila Ray, from *Poems from India*, by Daisy Alden, published by Thomas Y Crowell Company 1969, by permission of Mrs. J. Das to whom rights have reverted.

Dennis Donahue: "The Tortoise-Shell Spy," by permission of the author.

Babette Deutsch: "Black Panther" and Lioness Asleep" from *The Collected Poems of Babette Deutsch*, published by Doubleday & Company, Inc., copyright © 1969 by Babette Deutsch, by permission of the author to whom rights have reverted.

Doubleday & Company, Inc.: "mehitabel finds a home" from *The Lives and Times of Archy and Mehitabel*, by Don Marquis, copyright © 1927 by Don Marquis; "The Thing About Cats" from *No Place for Hiding*, by John L'Heureux, copyright © 1970 by Texas Quarterly; "Incident with Lions" from *A Footing on This Earth*, by Sara Henderson Hay, copyright © 1961 by Sara Henderson Hay; "Bush" from *The Shade-Seller*, by Josephine Jacobsen, copyright © 1974 by Josephine Jacobsen. All four poems reprinted by permission of Doubleday & Company, Inc.

E. P. Dutton & Co., Inc. "What the Gray Cat Sings" from *I Sing the Pioneer*, by Arthur Guiterman, copyright © 1936 E. P. Dutton, renewed 1953 by Vida Lindo Guiterman, reprinted by permission of Vida Lindo Guiterman, to whom all rights have reverted.

John Gray: "On a Cat Ageing" from *Gossip*, by Alexander Gray, published by Porpoise Press (Faber and Faber Ltd., agent), by permission of John Gray to whom all rights have reverted.

Farrar, Straus & Giroux, Inc.: "Midwife Cat," "December Cats," and "The Cat and the Miser" from *Collected and New Poems*, by Mark Van Doren, copyright © 1963 by Mark Van Doren. "Little Girl Cat" from *Dinosaurs and Violins*, by Hy Sobiloff, copyright © 1954 by Hy Sobiloff. "The Happy Cat" and "The Snow Leopard" from *The Complete Poems*, by Randall Jarrell, copyright © 1945 by Randall Jarrell, copyright © 1969 by Mrs. Randall Jarrell. All poems reprinted with the permission of Farrar, Straus & Giroux, Inc.

Emilie Glen: "Cat Ballerina Assoluta" from *Golden Year of the PSA Anthology*, Fine Editions Press, copyright © 1960 by Emilie Glen, by permission of the author.

Faber and Faber Limited: "The Naming of Cats" and "The Ad-dressing of Cats" from *Old Possum's Book of Practical Cats* by T. S. Eliot; "The Death of a Cat" from *The Collected Poems of Louis MacNiece*, Canadian rights only.

Grove Press: "Cat's Dream" from *Pablo Neruda: A New Decade (Poems 1958–1967)*, by Pablo Neruda, copyright © 1969 by Grove Press, Inc., by permission of Grove Press, Inc.

Harcourt Brace Jovanovich, Inc.: "The Naming of Cats" and "The Ad-dressing of Cats" from *Old Possum's Book of Practical Cats*, by T.S. Eliot, copyright © 1939, by T. S. Eliot, renewed 1967, by Esme Valerie Eliot. Reprinted by permission of Harcourt Brace Jovanovich, Inc.

Harper & Row: "The Jaguar" from *The Hawk in the Rain*, by Ted Hughes, copyright © 1957 by Ted Hughes. "Cats" from *Flowers of Evil*, by Charles Baudelaire, translated by George Dillon and Edna St. Vincent Millay, copyright © 1936 by George Dillon and Edna St. Vincent Millay. By permission of Harper & Row, publishers, Inc.

Harper's Magazine: "Ah How My Cat Benjamin" by Pauline M. Leet, copyright © 1957 by Harper's Magazine. Reprinted from the March 1957 issue by special permission.

Hawthorn Books, Inc.: "A Cat May Look at a King" from *Merry Go Round*, by Laura E. Richards, copyright 1935 by Laura E. Richards, copyright renewed © 1963 by Rosalind Richards and John Richards. Reprinted by permission of Hawthorn Books, Inc.

The Hogarth Press Ltd.: "Black Cat" from *New Poems* by Rainer Maria Rilke, Canadian rights only, courtesy of St. John's College, Oxford, and The Hogarth Press.

Houghton Mifflin Company: "A Literary Cat" from *Nineteen Million Elephants and Other Poems,* by Helen Bevington, copyright © 1946, 1948, 1949 and 1950 by Helen Bevington. "Cat," from *The Adventures of Tom Bombadil*, by J. R. R. Tolkien, copyright © 1962 by George Allen & Unwin Ltd. Both poems reprinted by permission of Houghton Mifflin Company.

Household Magazine: "The Too Fat Cat" by Elaine V. Emans, copyright 1936 by Arthur Capper. Household is no longer published.

Kaleidograph: "The Beast Within" by Jean Sewell Standish, April 1955. "Cat From the Night" by Hortense Roberta Roberts, October 1951, by permission of the author. Kaleidograph is no longer published.

James Kirkup: "The Bird Fancier" from *Refusal to Conform* published by Oxford University Press, copyright © 1963 by James Kirkup to whom all rights have reverted. Originally published in *The New Yorker* June 24, 1961. "The Kitten in the Falling Snow" by permission of the author. "To Puffin, A White Cat" from *A Correct Compassion & Other Poems* published by Oxford University Press, copyright © 1952 by James Kirkup to whom all rights have reverted, by permission of the author.

Bertha Klausner Literary Agency: "Cat" from *I Like Animals,* by Dorothy Baruch, copyright © 1963 by Harper & Brothers, reprinted by permission of Bertha Klausner International Literary Agency.

Kayak Books, Inc.: "Lines for a Favorite Cat" from *Under Orion,* by Eric Barker, copyright © 1970 by Eric Barker, by permission of Kayak Books, Inc.

Little, Brown and Company: "The Lion" from *Versus*, by Ogden Nash, copyright © 1944 by Ogden Nash. "The Cat" from *Many Long Years*

Ago, by Ogden Nash, copyright © 1933 by Ogden Nash. "The Panther" from *Verses From 1929 On*, by Ogden Nash, copyright © 1940 by Curtis Publishing Company. "Moon" from *Laughing Time*, by William Jay Smith, copyright © 1955 by William Jay Smith. All poems reprinted by permission of Little, Brown and Company.

David Bennett Laing: "The Great Alien" and "Miao" from *The Collected Poems of Dilys Laing*, published by The Press of Case Western Reserve University, copyright © 1967 Estate of Dilys Laing by David Bennett Laing. By permission of Alexander Laing, Administrator of the Estate of Dilys Laing.

J. B. Lippincott Company: "In Honour of Taffy Topaz" from *Songs for a Little House*, by Christopher Morley, copyright © 1917 by Christopher Morley, copyright renewed © 1945 by Christopher Morley. "Chang McTang McQuarter Cat," "My Cat, Mrs. Lick-A-Chin," and "How To Tell a Tiger" from *You Read to Me, I'll Read to You*, by John Ciardi, copyright © 1962 by John Ciardi. "Cats and Kings" from *Collected Poems* (In One Volume), by Alfred Noyes, copyright © 1906, renewed 1934 by Alfred Noyes. All poems reprinted by permission of J. B. Lippincott Company.

Macmillan Publishing Co., Inc.: "The Cat and the Moon" and "Two Songs of a Fool" from *Collected Poems*, by William Butler Yeats, copyright 1919 by Macmillan Publishing Co., Inc. renewed 1947 by Bertha Georgie Yeats. "Peter" from *Collected Poems*, by Marianne Moore, copyright 1935 by Marianne Moore, renewed © 1963 by Marianne Moore and T. S. Eliot. "The Wind and the Rain," "On a Night of Snow," "Portrait of a Young Cat" from *Night and the Cat*, by Elizabeth Coatsworth, copyright 1950 by Macmillan Publishing Co., Inc. "The Lion" and "The Mysterious Cat" from *Collected Poems*, by Vachel Lindsay, copyright 1914 by Macmillan Publishing Co., Inc. "Epitaph for My Cat" from *New and Selected Poems*, by Jean Garrigue, copyright © Jean Garrigue 1964. "Last Words to a Dumb Friend" from *Collected Poems*, by Thomas Hardy, copyright 1925 by Macmillan Publishing Co., Inc. "The Tigress" and "Quorum Porum" from *Collected Poems*, by Ruth Pitter, copyright © 1968 by Ruth Pitter. All poems reprinted by permission of Macmillan Publishing Co., Inc.

The Macmillan Company of Canada Limited: "The Prize Cat" from *Collected Poems*, by E. J. Pratt, edited by Northrop Frye, 1958 (second edition), reprinted by permission of The Macmillan Company of Canada Limited.

Michigan Quarterly Review: "The Perfect Lion" by Harold Witt, copyright © 1968 by University of Michigan, by permission of Michigan Quarterly Review.

Mary Britton Miller: "Cat" from *Menagerie* by Mary Britton Miller, copyright © 1928 by Macmillan Co., by permission of the author to whom rights have reverted.

New Directions Publishing Corporation: "The Lost Black-and-White Cat" from *With Eyes at the Back of Our Heads*, by Denise Levertov, copyright © 1959 by Denise Levertov Goodman. "Lion" from "A Bestiary," from *Collected Shorter Poems*, by Kenneth Rexroth, copyright © 1963 by Kenneth Rexroth. "Black Cat" from *New Poems*, by Rainer Maria Rilke, copyright The Hogarth Press Ltd. 1964. "Poem" from *Collected Earlier Poems*, by William Carlos Williams, copyright © 1938 by New Directions Publishing Corporation. "The Young Cat and the Chrysanthemums" from *Collected Later Poems*, by William Carlos Williams, copyright © 1950 by William Carlos Williams. All poems reprinted by permission of New Directions Publishing Corporation.

The New Yorker Magazine, Inc.: "Looking for Itsy" by Naomi Lazard, reprinted by permission; © 1971 The New Yorker Magazine, Inc. "Walking with Lulu in the Wood" by Naomi Lazard, reprinted by permission; © 1969 The New Yorker Magazine, Inc. "Catalog" by Rosalie Moore, reprinted by permission; © 1940, 1968 The New Yorker Magazine, Inc. "Winter Tryst" by Ormonde de Kay, reprinted by permission; © 1958 The New Yorker Magazine, Inc.

The New York Times: "Look, See the Cat" by Nancy Price, February 24, 1964, copyright © 1964, by permission of The New York Times and the author. "Conceit with Aunties, Urn and Puss" by Michael T. Leech, November 21, 1966, copyright © 1966, by permission of The New York Times.

W. W. Norton & Company, Inc.: "Cabal of Cat and Mouse" from *Nonsequences* by Christopher Middleton, copyright © 1961, 1962, 1963, 1964, 1965 by Christopher Middleton. "The Great Cats and the Bears" from *A Private Mythology*, by May Sarton, copyright © 1966 by May

Sarton. Both poems by permission of the authors and W. W. Norton & Company, Inc.

Harold Ober Associates Incorporated: "Cats" from *The Children's Bells* (published by Henry C. Walck, Inc.), by Eleanor Farjeon, copyright © 1960 by Eleanor Farjeon. "The Little Cats" from *The Stairway of Surprise* (published by Alfred A. Knopf, Inc.) by William Rose Benet, copyright © 1947 by William Rose Benet.

October House Inc.: "The Drunkard to His Gelded Cat" from *Ribs of Death*, by Paul Zimmer, copyright © 1967 by Paul Zimmer. "And I Will Consider My Cat Caitlin" from *Looking for Water* by Eric Barker, copyright © 1964 by Eric Barker. Both poems reprinted by permission of October House Inc.

Oxford University Press: "The Fisher Cat" © 1971 The New Yorker Magazine, Inc., from *Fields of Grace*, by Richard Eberhart, copyright © 1972 by Richard Eberhart. "The Death of a Cat" from *The Collected Poems of Louis MacNeice*, edited by E. R. Dodds, copyright © The Estate of Louis MacNeice 1966. "Old Tom" from *The Quarry*, by Richard Eberhart, copyright © 1964 by Richard Eberhart. "Concord Cats" from *Collected Poems 1930–1960*, by Richard Eberhart, copyright © 1960 by Richard Eberhart. All poems reprinted by permission of Oxford University Press, Inc.

Random House, Inc.: "The Cat in the Wood" from *Actfive and Other Poems*, by Archibald MacLeish, copyright 1948 by Archibald MacLeish, reprinted by permission of Random House, Inc. "The Rabbit as King of the Ghosts" from *The Collected Poems of Wallace Stevens*, copyright 1942 by Wallace Stevens and renewed © 1970 by Holly Stevens, reprinted by permission of Alfred A. Knopf, Inc. "A Domestic Cat" by Edwin Denby from *An Anthology of New York Poets*, edited by Ron Padgett and David Shapiro, copyright © 1970 by Random House, Inc., reprinted by permission of the publisher.

Raymond Roseliep: "Calico June," by permission of the author.

Alan Ross: "Zoo" from *Poems 1942–67*, published by Eyre & Spottiswood Ltd., 1967, by permission of the author to whom all rights have reverted.

Saturday Review Co.: "Dr. Faustus to His Cat" by Anne Young, first appeared in Saturday Review October 27, 1951, copyright 1951 by Saturday Review Co. Used with permission. "The Innkeeper's Cat" by Ulrich Troubetzkoy, first appeared in Saturday Review December 25, 1948, copyright 1948 by Saturday Review Co. Used with permission of both Saturday Review and author. "Honey from the Lion" by Leah Bodine Drake, first appeared in Saturday Review December 6, 1947, copyright 1947 by Saturday Review Co., used with permission.

Naomi Replansky: "The Ratless Cat" from *Ring Song*, published by Charles Scribner's Sons, copyright 1952 by Charles Scribner's Sons, reprinted with permission of the author to whom all rights have reverted. I. L. Salomon: "Ballad for a Coal-Black Tom" from *Unit & Universe*, published by Clarke & Way, copyright © 1959 by I. L. Salomon, reprinted by permission of the author to whom all rights have reverted.

May Sarton: "Tiger" from *The Land of Silence*, published by Rinehart & Company, Inc., copyright 1953 by May Sarton, by permission of the author to whom all rights have reverted.

Charles Scribner's Sons: "The Black Panther" from *Poems From Three Decades*, by Richmond Lattimore, copyright 1951 Richmond Lattimore. "The Lion" from *The Treasure Ship*, by Herbert Asquith, copyright 1926 Charles Scribner's Sons. "Requiescat" from *By Daylight and in Dream*, by John Hall Wheelock, copyright © 1970 John Hall Wheelock. "Waiting for *IT*" (copyright 1957 May Swenson); "Cat and the Weather" (copyright © 1963 May Swenson); "The Lion" (copyright 1957 May Swenson) from *To Mix With Time* by May Swenson. "Drawing the Cat" (copyright © 1965 May Swenson); "The Secret in the Cat" (copyright © 1964 as "His Secret" May Swenson) from *Poems to Solve* by May Swenson. All poems reprinted by permission of Charles Scribner's Sons.

Sheed & Ward, Ltd.: "The Pets" from *This Man was Ireland*, by Robert Farren, copyright 1943 by Sheed & Ward, by permission of Sheed & Ward, Ltd.

Pearl Andelson Sherry: "Cats" published in The Forge, autumn 1927, by permission of the author.

Sidgwick & Jackson Ltd.: "India" from *The Hunter and Other Poems*, by W. J. Turner, copyright 1916 by W. J. Turner; "A Garden Lion" from *A Garden in the Antipodes* by Evelyn Hayes, copyright 1929 by Evelyn Hayes, by permission of the authors and Sidgwick & Jackson Ltd.

Simon & Schuster, Inc.: "A Cat" by John Gittings from *Miracles*, edited by Richard Lewis, copyright 1966 by Richard Lewis, by permission of Simon & Schuster, Inc. "The Tiger" from *Tiger of Time*, by C. F. MacIntyre, copyright © 1965 by C. F. MacIntyre, reprinted by permission of Trident Press, division of Simon & Schuster, Inc.

Slawson Communications, Inc.: for permission to reprint the following poems from Cat Fancy, copyright 1970, 1971, 1972, 1973, 1974: "Tom Peeper" by Francis Maguire, "The Cat Whose Name is Mouse" by Joanne de Longchamps, "Cats" by Robert Gibb, "The City Cats" by Bruce H. Guernsey, "The Old Cat" by Frank Finale, "Cat" by Ruth Graydon, "Storm" by Daisy Stieber Squadra, "Return of the Prodigal" by Frances Minturn Howard, "Elegy for a Black Cat" by May Sarton, "Emmycat" by Catherin Young, "Watchcat" by Mimi Drake, "The Cat" by Ann Stanford, "Mrs. Vandegrift" by Dorothy Hughes, "One's Own Lion" by Norma Farber, "Charade" by Aline Beveridge, "One for a Guy Who was a Cat" by Nancy G. Westerfield, "Two Sick Kittens" by May Sarton, "Marmalade Lost" by Ruth Whitman, "The Cat Named Colette" by Joanne de Longchamps, "In Winter" by George MacBeth, "Vagabond Prince" by Anne Barlow, "Kitten" by Raymond Holden, "Communication" by Jennie Palen, "Procession" by Norma Farber, "Polka Dot" by David Locher, "The Artist Sketches One Cat" by Elizabeth Yungul, "New Cat" by Lisl Auf der Heide, "The Cat in the Window" by Harry Humes, "Cat at Night" by Harry Humes, "Tipsy" by Emilie Glen, "Animals Want to Know" by George Keithley, "For One Who lives with Me" by Francis Maguire, "Sleeping Cats" by Jean Pedrick, "Cinnamon the Cat" by Hortense Roberta Roberts, "Symposium" and "A Certain Wisdom" by Ruth Munch, "Cat" by George Barr, "Dialogue" by Evelyn Ames, "The Cat" by Philip Dacey, "Radar Screen" by Jean Harper, "Villanelle for the Cat" by Philip Dacey, "My Cat with His Butterfly Eyes" by Donald Finkel and Constance Urdang (originally appeared under pseudonym of D. F. Chuff), "Tigger" by H. McAden Burwell, "Cantaloupe Cat" by Bernice Ames, "Two Cats" by Jean Harper, "Cat Chasing the Fly" by T. J. Worthington, "The Cat Ballet" by Eve Triem, "At the Lion Cage" by Oliver Hale, "The Lion in the Willow" by Norma Farber, "Look You're Laughing" by George Keithley, "Stalked" by Jerene Cline, '"Snow Leopard" by Harold Witt, "To Speak to a Lion" by Jean Harper, "Captive Lions" by Harold Witt, "The Forum on Friday" by Daisy Stieber Squadra, "Cat on a Holiday" by Nancy G. Westerfield, "In a Hotel Lobby" by Hortense

Roberta Roberts, "Charlie's Legs" by Eleanor B. Zimmerman, "Pullman Cat" by Nancy G. Westerfield, and "Unquestionably Cat" by A. D. Freeman.

William Jay Smith: "Cat," "Tiger," "Lion" from *Boy Blue's Book of Beasts,* published by Atlantic-Little, Brown, copyright © 1957 by William Jay Smith, reprinted by permission of William Jay Smith, to whom rights have reverted.

Society of Authors: "Double Dutch," "Comfort" and "Five Eyes" by Walter de la Mare, reprinted by permission of Literary Trustees of Walter de la Mare and Society of Authors as their representative.

Southern Review: "For a Yellow Cat at Midnight" by Jean Burden, copyright May 29, 1971 by Jean Burden, reprinted with her permission. Allan Swallow Press, Inc.: "Death of a Cat" from *Private Dooms and Public Destinations: Poems 1945–1962,* by James Schevill, copyright © 1960, 1962 by James Schevill, by permission of The Swallow Press, Chicago.

United Church Herald: "Indoor Jungle Blues" by Ulrich Troubetzkoy, which appeared in the issue of June 1970, by permission of the author. University of California Press: "Alcoholic Lion" from *Collected Poems 1915–1967,* by Kenneth Burke, copyright © 1968 by Kenneth Burke.

"The Panther" from *RAINER M. RILKE: Selected Poems,* translated by C. F. MacIntyre, published 1940. Both poems reprinted by permission of The Regents of the University of California.

University of Michigan Press: "Extinct Lions" from *Fingers of Hermes* by Radcliffe Squires, copyright © 1965 by University of Michigan Press, reprinted by permission of the publisher and the author.

University of Nebraska Press: "Colloquy" from *The Collected Poems of Weldon Kees,* copyright © 1960 by John A. Kees. Originally published in The New Yorker.

Viking Press, Inc.: "The Cat on the Mat Deserves a Pat" from *Times Three* by Phyllis McGinley, copyright © 1955 by Phyllis McGinley. Originally apepared in The New Yorker. Reprinted by permission of The Viking Press, Inc. "Spanish Lions" from *Times Three* by Phyllis McGinley, copyright © 1958 by Phyllis McGinley. Reprinted by permission of The Viking Press, Inc.

Wesleyan University Press: "Cat on Couch" from *Light and Dark* by Barbara Howes, copyright © 1955 by Barbara Howes. "The Captive Lion" and "The Cat" from *The Complete Poems of W. H. Davies*, copyright © 1963 by Jonathan Cape, Ltd. All three poems reprinted by permission of Wesleyan University Press.

Yankee, Inc.: for permission to reprint the following poems from Yankee Magazine, published in Dublin, New Hampshire, copyright 1956, 1958, 1962, 1967, 1968, 1969, 1970, 1974.

"Vignette of Summer" by Frances Minturn Howard, "Death of the Black Cat, Mr. Jingle" by Frances Minturn Howard, "A Troubled Sleep" by Eric Barker, "Ocelot" by Bernice Ames, "Cats" by Joanne de Longchamps, "In Connecticut, There are Cats" by Betty Lowry, "On Dino, My Cat, Who Flew Across the Continent" by Karen Rose, "Death of the Kitchen Cat" by Nancy G. Westerfield, "Sea Cats at Dusk" by Bianca Bradbury, and "If Cats Don't Go to Heaven, What Will the Angels String Their Harps With?" by Myron H. Broomell.

INDEX